# Dissecting America's Most Lawless President

## BY FEGGO & HENRY KAUFMAN

# Introduction

It will be four years ago in September that we started this Trump cartoon journey.

Our first cartoon series was titled: "TrumpTruth" and was subtitled "Dissecting America's Most Dishonest President." For some reason we felt that falsity versus truth was a distinguishing feature of Donald Trump as America's 45th President.

Cartoons in the TrumpTruth book covered a nearly 2-year period from 9/13/20 through 8/20/22. Or, in other words, from less than two months before the 2020 Presidential election – which Trump would falsely label a "landslide" victory for himself – to a bit more than two months before the 2022 Midterms, when Republican hopes were again soundly rejected.

The point of the TrumpTruth cartoons – and then the book – was to illuminate – as only well-targeted humor can – what had really been going on during Trump's four years as the 45th President of the United States; followed by the 2020 election – which Trump lost but denied losing – and thus also closely covering the run-up to Trump's January 6 insurrection and its aftermath. And finally leaving off shortly before the 2022 Midterm disaster for the Republicans and – in particular – for most MAGA election deniers.

* * * * * *

Following on the TrumpTruth book, came nonstop fodder for this second, TrumpLaw book, subtitled "Dissecting America's Most Lawless President." Of course, as it turned out, there was also no truth whatever to a boatload of events and activities also perfectly-described under the title "TrumpLaw."

And of course, as followers of the news readily observed, from the point of view of Donald Trump himself, as candidate again now for the 47th Presidency, TrumpLaw actually translated very neatly into the much abused claim of "election interference!" However, as we pointed out in any number of our responsive Trump cartoons, the originator and source of what Trump was manipulatively calling: "election interference," was actually Donald Trump himself!! Or, in other words, what could possibly be greater "election interference" than sending a mob of insurrectionists to our hallowed national capitol building to disrupt the constitutionally and legally-mandated counting of state-certified electoral college votes on the very day appointed for that event.

If more explanation is needed, the "election interference" that Donald Trump was purporting to decry – carefully analyzed and understood – was actually nothing more than the inevitable, legal follow-up to the original, Trump-initiated "election interference" and related events, into which Trump had thrown himself immediately after the 2020 election eve – and even well before – for which Donald Trump was undeniably responsible. And only thereafter – quite appropriately – was Trump's transparently lawless election interference and related at best legally-questionable activities pursued by authorities in various courts of law – state and federal, civil and criminal.

In the context of the foregoing, our Book #2, TrumpLaw, contains cartoons beginning just after the 2022 Midterm elections (11/17/22), and ending – appropriately – on April 1, 2024. I.e., April Fools' Day. With the only question remaining who exactly were this year's primary April fools? And, with more than half the year remaining before Election Day 2024. One can only marvel at the terrible and unprecedented adventures that lay ahead in the final 218 days of our country's heretofore honored election cycle!

AN ADDITIONAL NOTE: roughly the first two dozen cartoons reproduced in this book were originally published by our cartoon syndicator at that time, CartoonArts International. After that point we effectively declared our independence. So the balance of Book #2's cartoons were originally published on co-author Henry Kaufman's Twitter (and then later "X") account: @Henry_Kaufman20. Those posts also included much more extensive and robust, non-cartoon, editorial information and narrative of one kind or another, has had at the moment inspired this commentator.  And several of the post-Cartoons Arts toons were also republished to larger audiences – either in *the Nation* magazine, as chosen for its online "OppArt" section, or on David Cay Johnston's popular Twitter/X feed (@ DavidCayJ) reaching a bit under 200,000 followers.

*I once again dedicate this book to my loyal wife, Meryl Unger, our daughter Erica Kaufman Asher, my sister Carol Kaganov, and to all of our extended family, for their love and their kind support for my continuing sally into political cartooning.*
*Henry Kaufman*

*To Andrea Arroyo, Gracias for your advise and patience!*
*Feggo*

# Acknowledgements

Once again we can generally say that our Trump cartoon series, as well as this latest, TrumpLaw series, would not have been possible without the support and continuing counsel of Jens Robinson, President of Cartoon Arts International. He published all of our TrumpTruth cartoons and, as here indicated, also published the first two dozen or so of our new TrumpLaw cartoons. Sadly, we were unable to continue that relationship, and went forward on our own, still with great friendship and thanks for that early support. It was indispensable. And most appreciated.

Our Trump cartoons readership remains small but loyal. In addition, we once again have been honored to receive words of support from some notable readers and fans, including once again from friend and one-time client, David Cay Johnston, premier investigative journalist and book author and perhaps the most prominent expert on Donald Trump's tax and financial situation.

Finally, we have been honored, once again, to have a small number of our cartoons selected for republication by *the Nation Online* in their "OppArt" section.

ELECTION
2024
CARTOON
CALENDAR
©feggo & Kaufman 2024

1 Day to Election Day

This cartoon seems to be as good a way as any to lead off our second book of piling on to Trump, his handpicked "advisors" for a horror show "administration," with a massive dose of intended – or at least attempted – humor. Summing up a significant aspect of their terms in office – after they both had left the White House. Of course, these descriptions also serve to encapsulate what one can only imagine are the still-raw views of the President and Vice President after the dramatic and unprecedented end of their terms in office. And, in particular after the "insurrection" of January 6. The other contrast that stands out is the polar opposite views and attitudes and styles of the two men. While each does try to include something complementary, we can see the sharp differences between the two men in their ability to do so.

Two interesting additional notes: (i) Pence's final position, opposing Trump's second run for President – an opposing position implicit in the comments of Vice President Pence here – was in the end not made explicit for another year and five months – in fact not until March 15, 2024 – well into the primary season of the 2024 presidential election season! On the other hand, the strongly negative tone of defeated former President Trump's comments about his Vice President were predictably harsh. (A final note: this author must confess to experiencing one tiny bit of censorship directed at him – believe it or not – that was imposed by our newspaper cartoon syndicate – a media entity that must always be conscious of the range of ages of its readers.

But now, truth can be told, the fact of the matter is that Donald Trump did not refer to his Veep as merely a "wimp." The word he actually used – famously (and apparently one of Trump's favorites) – was that Pence was a "pussy!"

Published by Cartoon Arts International, 11/17/2022

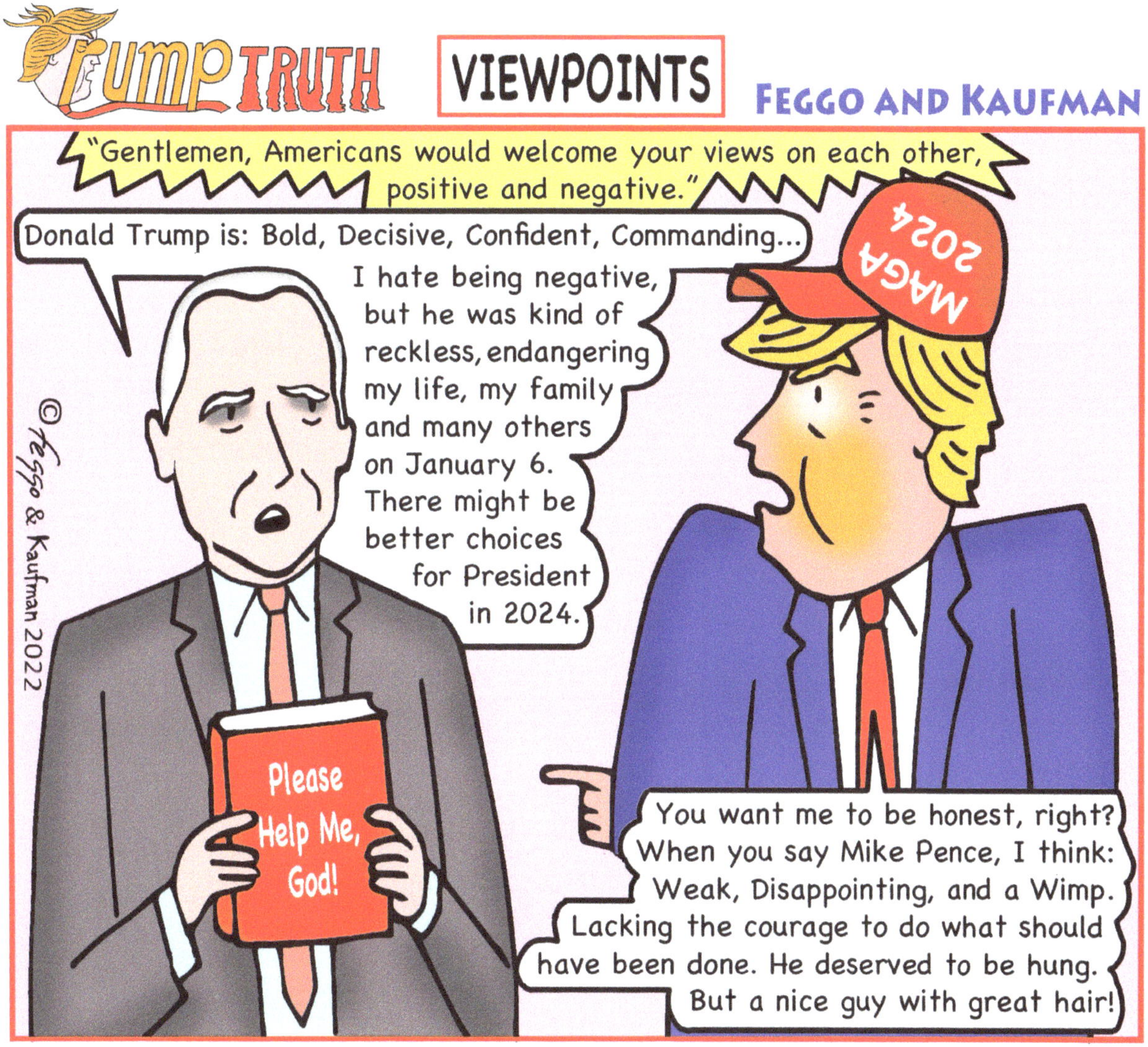

# TRUMP TRUTH — VIEWPOINTS — FEGGO AND KAUFMAN

Those closely following the trials and tribulations of the defeated former president, may recall that the news his candidacy immediately generated came far sooner than normal. Informed speculation theorized that – with all of his charges and indictments building up – Trump concluded that an uncommonly early candidacy might be a way to defeat such charges on the ground that a presidential candidate should not be subjected to the same rules as a normal person – or at least might not be!

So here we have Trump appearing to put forward a confident image recalling his – successful – first run for the presidency. Now, however, Trump's apparent bravado actually seems to be covering up some likely daunting inner doubts – at two extremes. I.e., will Trump – "alone" – find himself in the White House again in 2024? Or will he find himself – very truly "alone" – serving one or more long bids behind bars?

Published by Cartoon Arts International, 11/18/2022;

Republished by *the Nation Online*, "OppArt," 2/20/2023

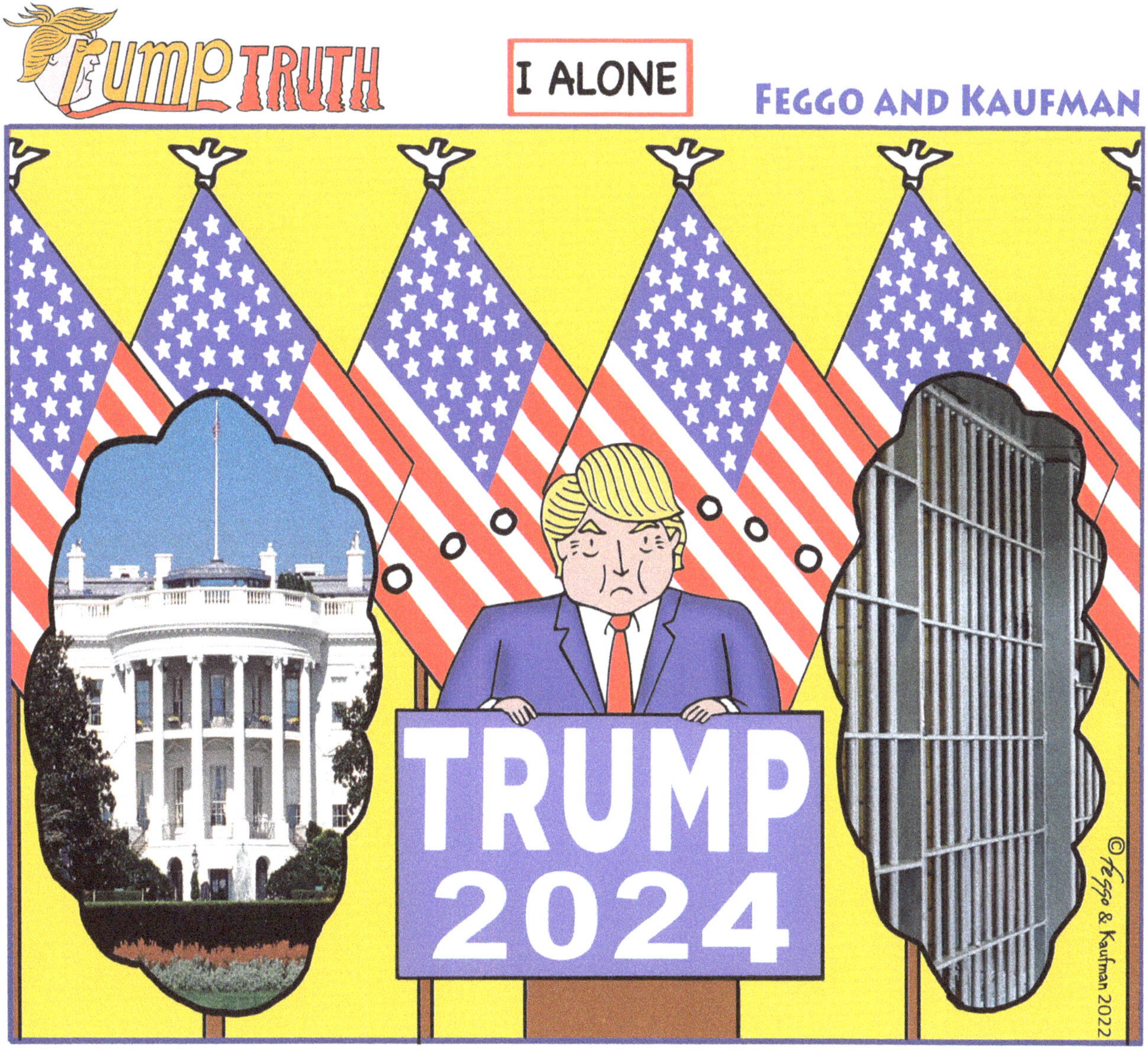

I ALONE

FEGGO AND KAUFMAN

If there were any single, derisive, label used – actually overused – by Trump during his
candidacies and presidency it was the expression "witch hunts." (In all likelihood "fake
news" came in a close second.) The "witch hunt" phrase was transparently intended by
Trump to diminish the constant legal or criminal charges or allegations being hurled
at him. Of course, overuse of any term of this sort soon undermines its novelty and
effectiveness. As proven by Trump's use of what ultimately became a more
and more stale buzzword less and less persuasive in his own defense.


Published by Cartoon Arts International, 1/15/2023

What are you in for?
© feggo & Kaufman 2023

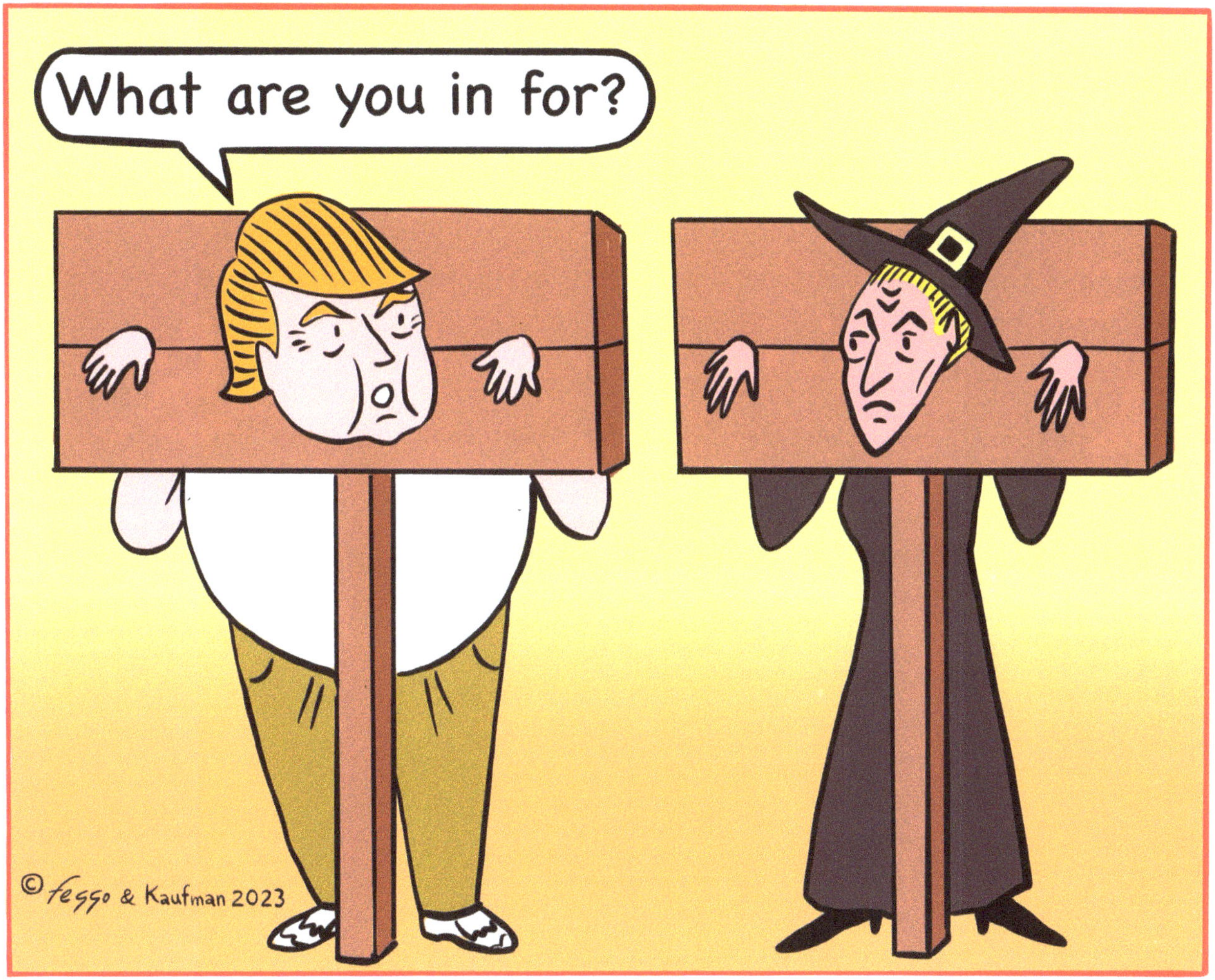

Donald Trump's idea of legal argumentation: affected eloquence and an attempt at oratorical persuasiveness, is here distilled into a single Trump-like summation related to the competing "classified" documents charges as against Trump and Biden. In this cartoon all of the elements of a typical Trumpian argument are deployed: a comparison between the claimed "perfection*" of his actions, in contrast to his adversary's obvious lack of same, is deployed to a jury already buttered up with Trump's over-the-top – not to be taken for sincere – but compliments.

*Here, you should think back to that "perfect" phone call to the Ukraine. And then also Trump's supposedly "perfect" phone call to the Georgia Secretary of State asking him to "find" a mere 11,780 additional votes for the otherwise indubitably losing candidate in that State.

Published by Cartoon Arts International, 1/22/2023

**FEGGO AND KAUFMAN**

By all accounts, Donald's relationship to his father, Fred Trump, is known to have had a deep, lasting – and by all accounts daunting if not destructive – impact on Donald. Here, we speculate on one of the lessons his father may well have given him which, if so, seems to have lasted a lifetime. Yet at least at the time it was given, little Donald appears to have been somewhat confused by the message his father was conveying. Still, that hard lesson was ultimately taken to heart and more and more frequently came in handy for Donald as he grew into a man!

Published by Cartoon Arts International, 1/30/2023; also published on Twitter @DavidCayJ, 1/26/23; and @henry_kaufman20, 1/30/23

# FEGGO AND KAUFMAN

Here is more heavy-duty lawyering by Donald Trump. This time addressing those pesky allegations (surely another "witch hunt") of a one-night (or less, possibly much, much less) stand, years ago with a porn star whose name appears to have predicted the shameful consequences of Donald's shameless act. But this time Trump resorts to name dropping other attorneys who had allegedly weighed in on the matter – or at least involved themselves in the post-matter payoff and related legal parsing. Clearly, Trump has already been briefed on the legalities, even relying on the claimed "tolling" of the statute of limitations on the charge during his four years in office as President of the United States.

Published by Cartoon Arts International, 2/4/2023

# TRUMP LAW

DJT 45



## FEGGO AND KAUFMAN

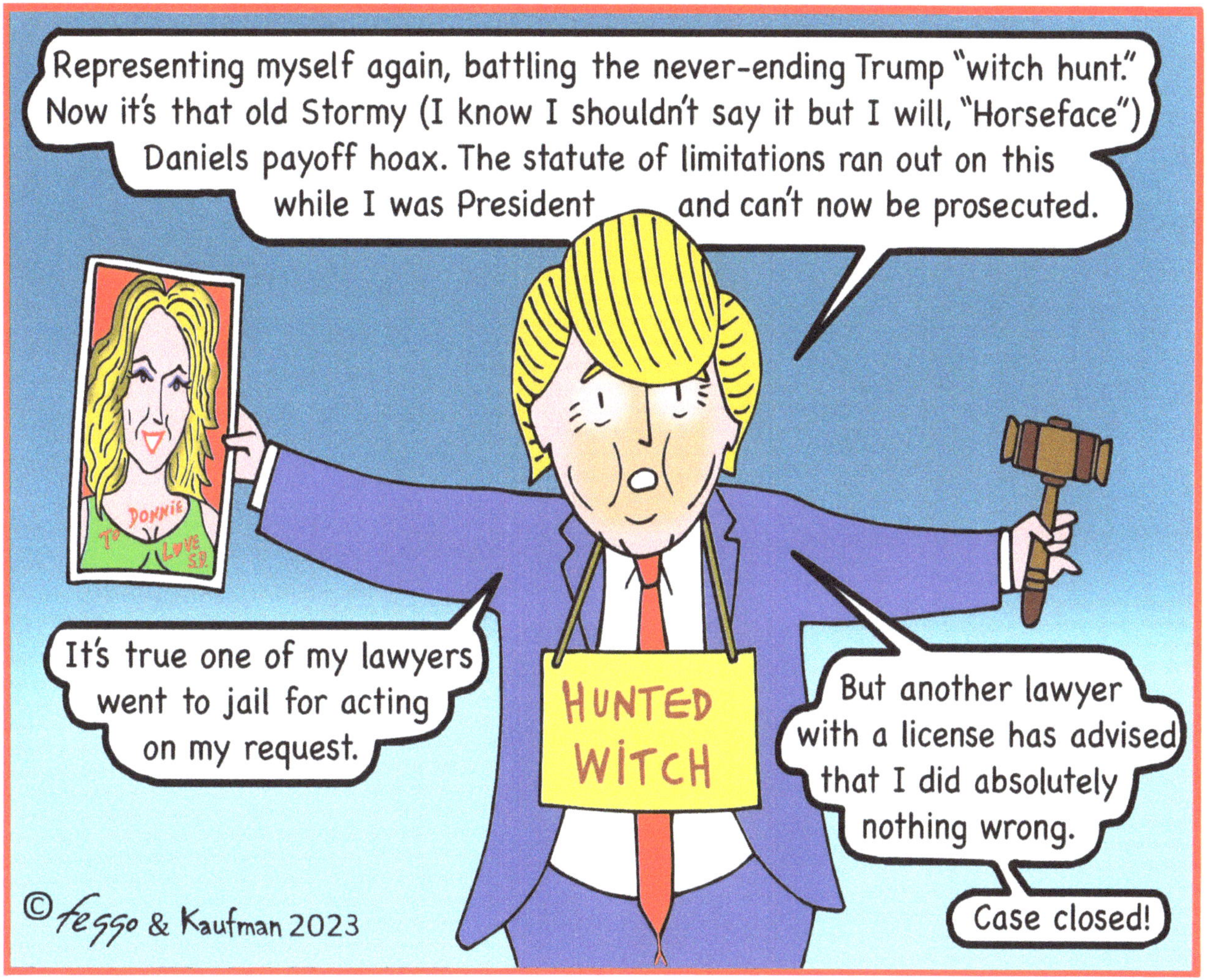

Speaking of legal "witch hunts," Donald once again finds himself in the weeds of serious criminal allegations, pro and con. For those who do not recall, Mark Pomerantz was brought in as special counsel to the New York District Attorney, examining potential criminal charges against Trump. A perfect opportunity for a rather thorough, classic Trumpian list of grievances, on the one hand, and ad hominem attacks, on the other. (An ironic additional side note: I believe Trump may never have connected the dots between one of his reviled "Democrat law firms in New York" and some of the other people at that law firm who intruded into his life. Ironically, this includes the no-nonsense U.S. District Judge Lewis Kaplan, the bane of Trump's existence at a future time when on trial against "Miss Bergdorf Goodman" in what ended up being her very, very expensive sexual assault and defamation claims against Donald. Present at that firm for a few years also includes yours truly, Henry Kaufman!

Published by Cartoon Arts International, 2/8/2023

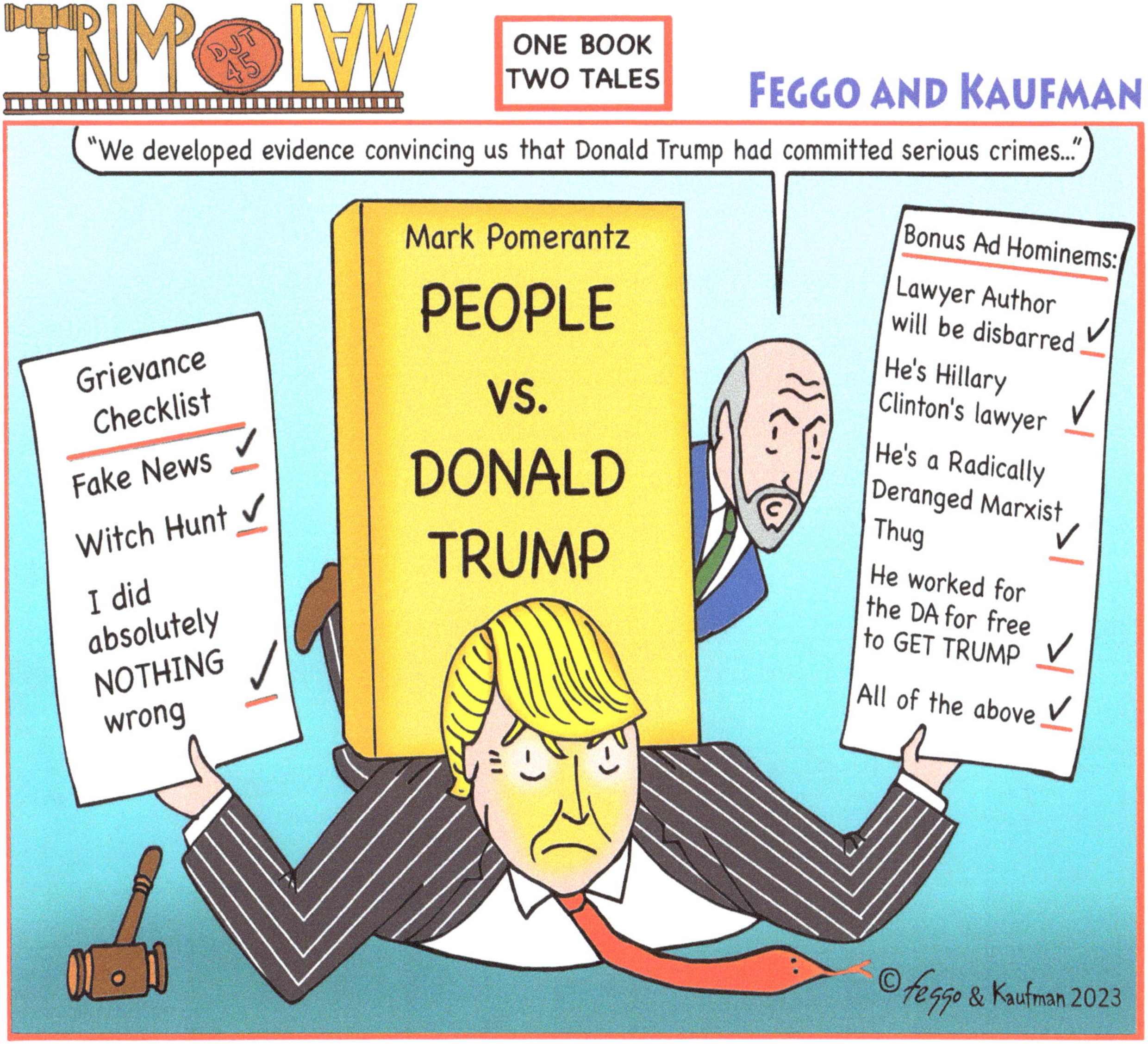

# FEGGO AND KAUFMAN

In connection with his many and unceasing legal travails, Donald Trump surely arrived at some very strong opinions – great or dismal – about his own attorneys. In this cartoon, Trump actually manages to speak admiringly of some "creative lawyering." Although it is also quite possible Trump has in mind here his own tactical brilliance as opposed to any single lawyer – paid or unpaid. Here, the other source of insight is, of all things, a student who finds himself at the "Trump Law School" (national ranking unknown). This It's amazing how students – even at such a modestly-ranked school – can sometimes manage to see through the clutter and come up with a brilliant insight. We might even suggest transferring to Harvard Law School, young man!

Published by Cartoon Arts International, 2/15/2023

# TRUMP LAW



# FEGGO AND KAUFMAN

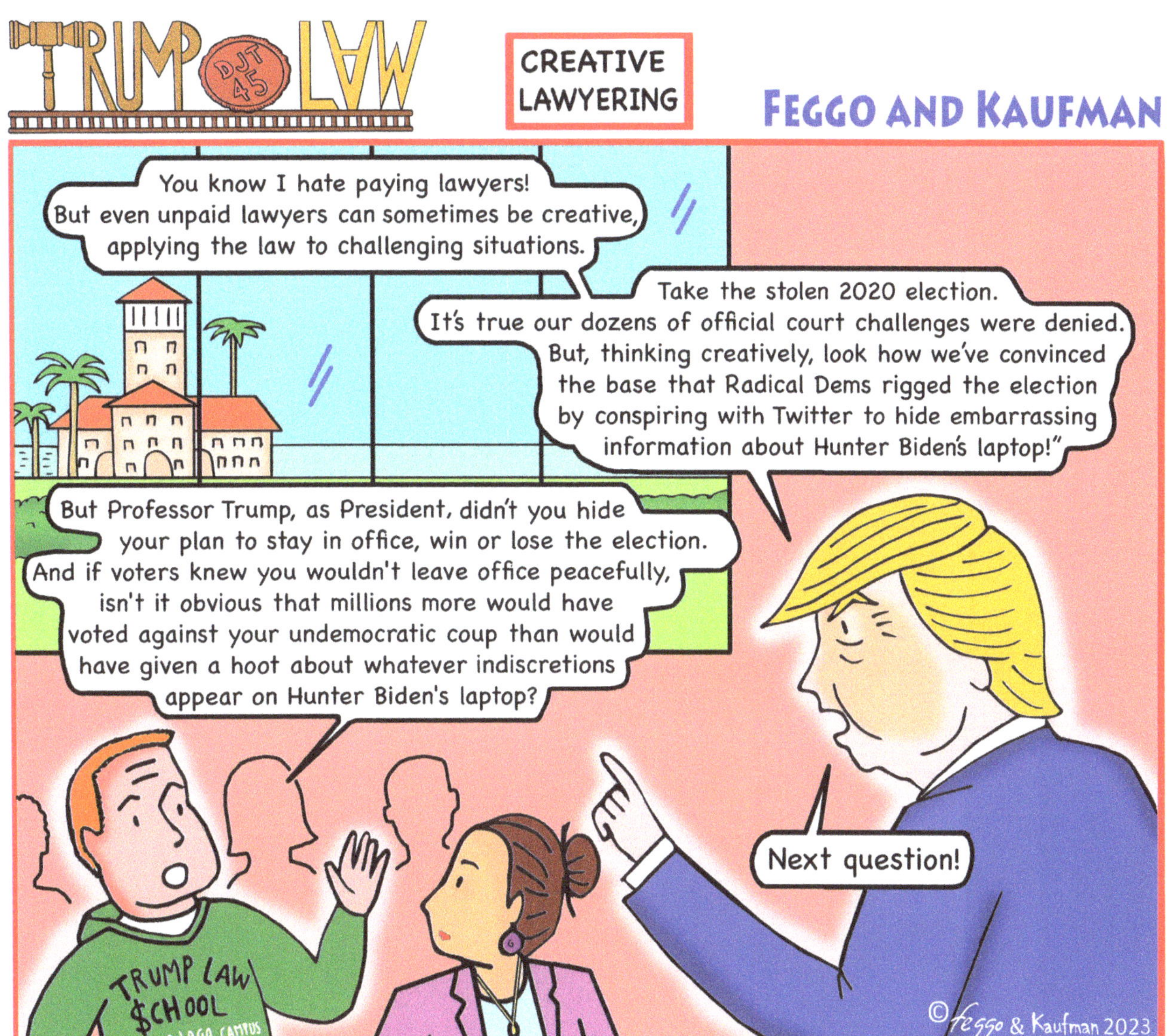

In the State of Georgia, Donald Trump seems to have leapt to some premature and overly optimistic conclusions about the results of a preliminary, Special Grand Jury proceeding. It seems that the sanctity of grand jury secrecy had led to Donald's rare positivity which – unfortunately for him – later turned out to be wrongheaded and baseless.

Published by Cartoon Arts International, 2/22/2023

PREMATURE EXONERATION

# FEGGO AND KAUFMAN

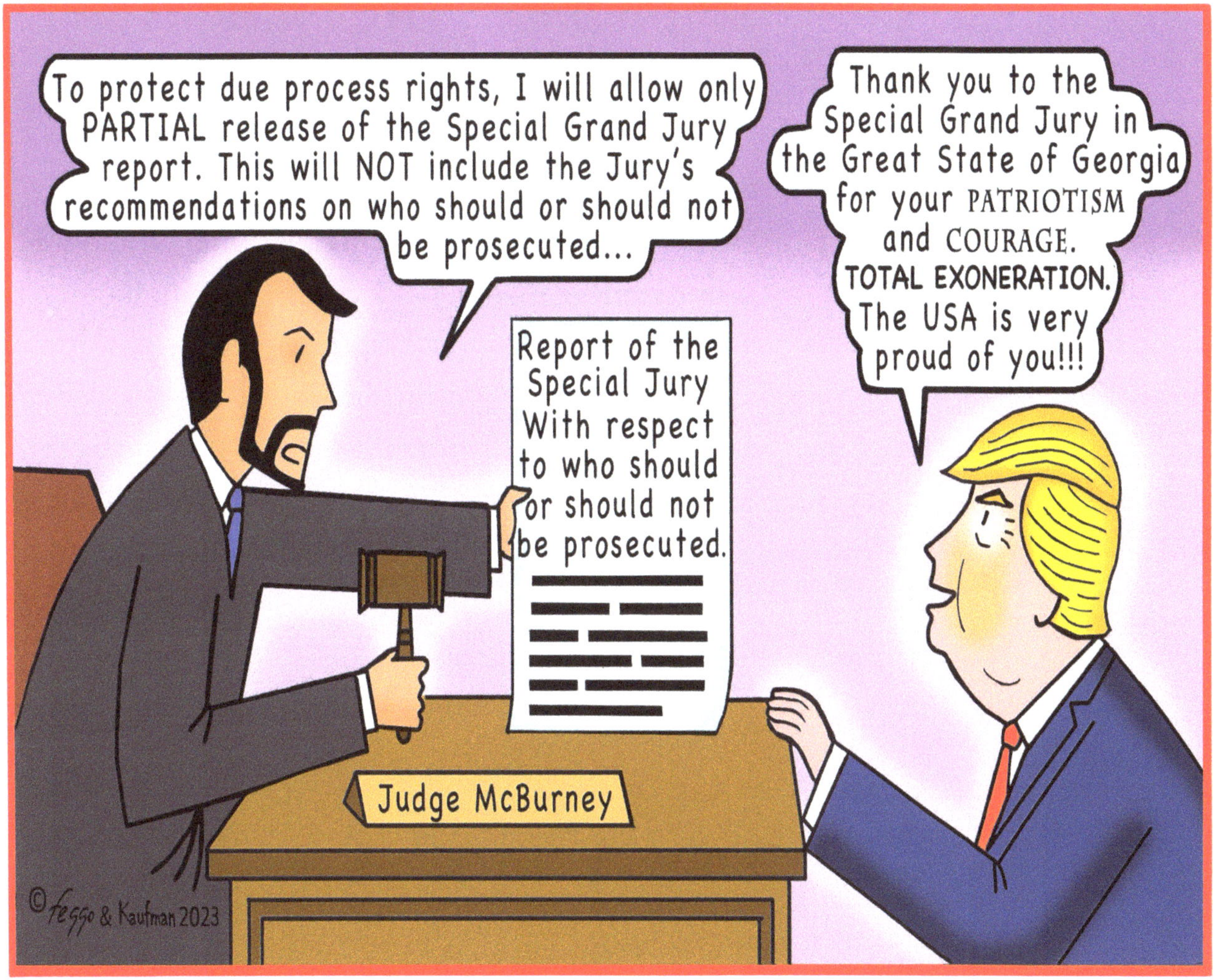

In similar mistaken fashion, it so happens that Donald Trump once again radically misunderstood what had transpired before and after the Georgia Special Grand Jury process. So here we see the world of extremes that Donald Trump lives in: the stark contrast between Donald's premature joy at what turned out not to be a vindication at all and then his typically dark and extreme view of anyone who is not completely supportive. And so, in Trump's all or nothing world, grand jurors who he had at first praised as "patriotic and courageous" thereafter immediately morphed into "Thugs" and Trump-haters."

Published by Cartoon Arts International, 2/25/2023

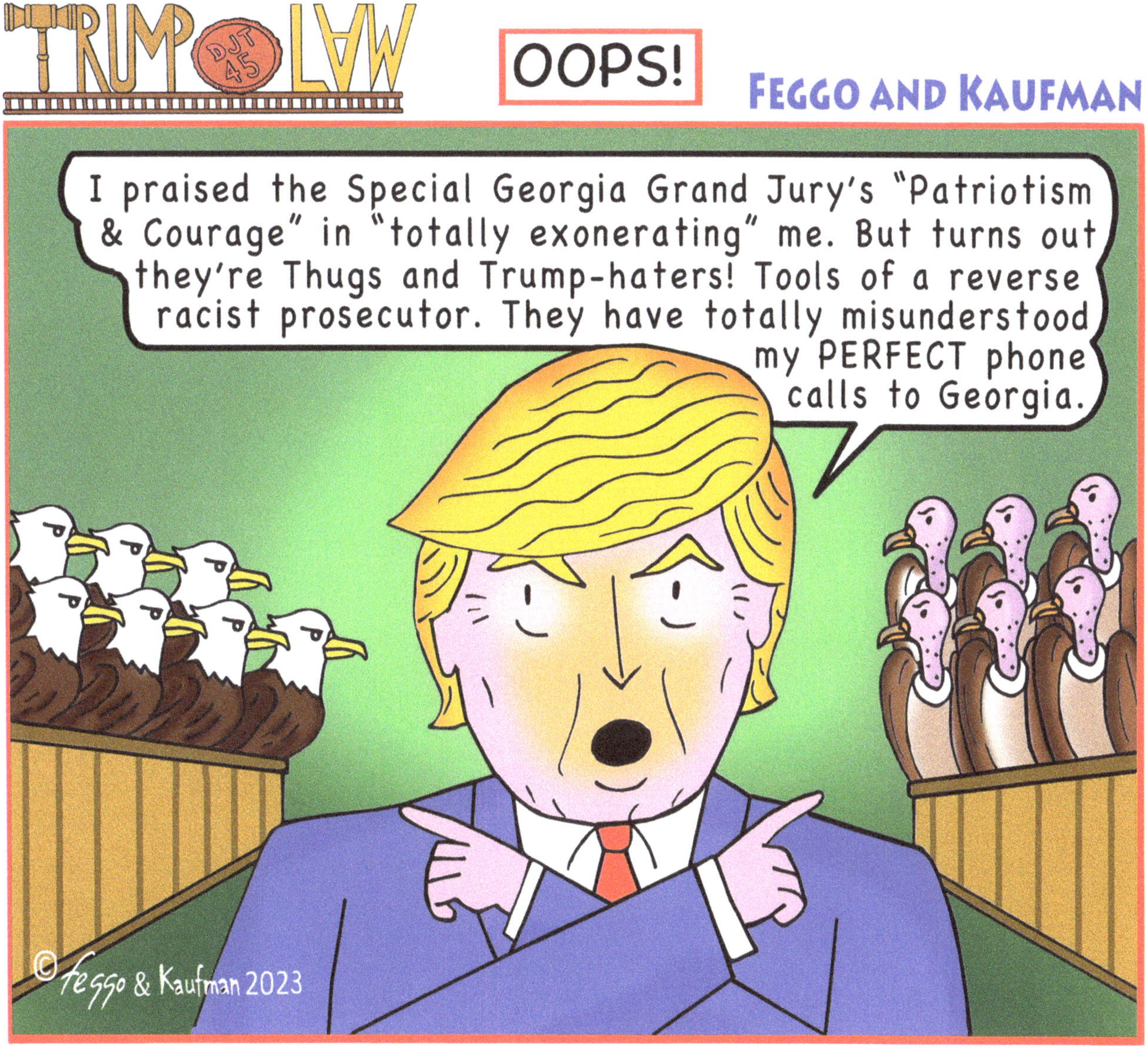

# FEGGO AND KAUFMAN

This "Double Jeopardy" cartoon is one of our simplest and most straightforward. All that it requires is buying into Donald Trump's upside down view of the world. For Trump it is simple: one "big lie" (2020) sets the stage for another almost equally big lie which is also a ready-made and prepackaged excuse for Trump's losing the 2024 election. Of course, it will come as no surprise to readers that, from the point of view of this author, Trump's unhappy "truth" in 2024 will be an especially welcome fact.

Published by Cartoon Arts International, 3/5/2023

TRUMP LAW
DJT 45
DOUBLE JEOPARDY
FEGGO AND KAUFMAN

They stole the 2020 election from me!
That spiteful loser and
her Unselect Committee.
Now the Trump-hating Special Counsel
wants to steal 2024
by prosecuting me for 2020!

After Trump's big lie,
all we want is the simple truth,
the whole truth,
and nothing but the truth.

We the People
Amendment V
No person shall be held to answer for a capital, or otherwise infamous crime, unless on a presentment or indictment of a Grand Jury, except in cases arising in the land or naval forces, or in the Militia, when in actual service in time of War or public danger; nor shall any person be subject for the same offence to be twice put in jeopardy of life or limb; nor shall be compelled in any criminal case to be a witness against himself, nor be deprived of life, liberty, or property without due process of law; nor shall private property be for public use, without just compensation.

JANUARY 6th REPORT

Feggo & Kaufman 2023

Diligent followers of our initial TrumpTruth cartoon book will recall that a few additional characters came into the book along the way. In particular, readers may recall our pair of humorous, politically-astute, pigeons – Plucky & Yacky – who arrived on the scene one very cold January day in New York's Union Square Park.
(Too complicated to explain here!)

Not to be outdone, for this TrumpLaw book, we have added a most apt pair of other birds, the "Legal Eagles." With one amusing side note: as a practicing attorney, trained at a leading New England law school, I was about to name our Legal Eagles something classically law-related – actually, "Holmes and Brandeis" had come immediately to mind.

Propitiously, the humor of the names of our feathered characters, this time, was saved in the nick of time by a much better idea, coming from my wonderful, longtime assistant, Kate Konigisor. She said, why be obscure with names having minimal general or immediate recognition?  For popular appeal, how about: "Perry & Mason"? As soon as I heard her suggestion I knew that pair would be the just perfect "Legal Eagles" for our TrumpLaw book! And if you're a stickler for details, as is our wonderful artist Feggo, take note that Legal Eagle Mason wears a pair of spectacles and a bow tie, as seems appropriate for such a dedicated legal scholar! And, as you'll see, much like real practicing attorneys, neither Perry nor Mason has much patience for Trump's inattention to sound legal advice!!

Published by Cartoon Arts International, 3/10/2023

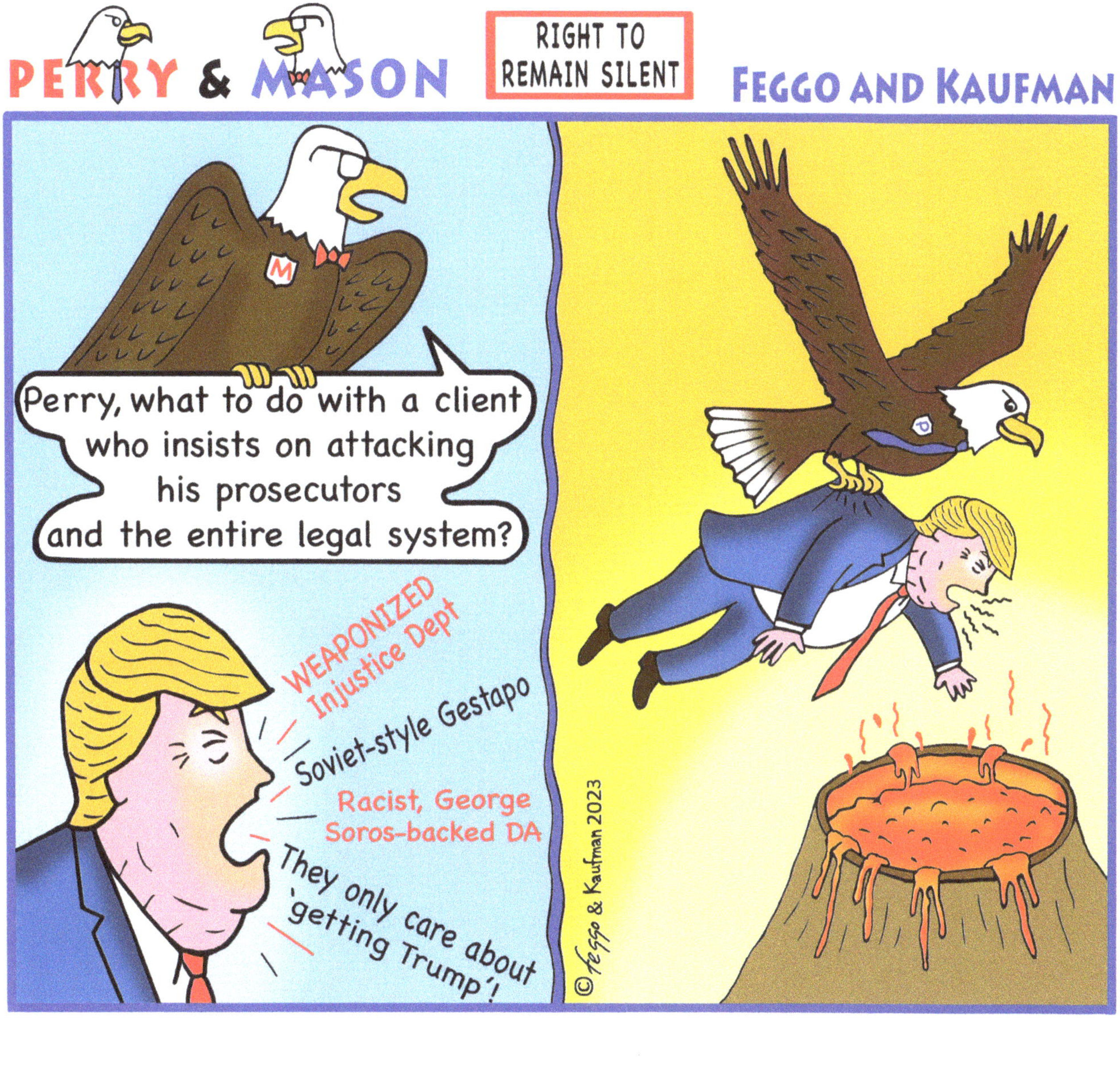

Perry, what to do with a client who insists on attacking his prosecutors and the entire legal system?

WEAPONIZED Injustice Dept

Soviet-style Gestapo

Racist, George Soros-backed DA

They only care about 'getting Trump'!

© Feggo & Kaufman 2023

Donald Trump has not been shy about signaling to both his supporters and adversaries some of the startling things he has in mind for the country should he be elected to a second term in office. Followers of Trump and/or the news know that high up on Trump's list is one constant theme – indeed, unabashed warning – of the "retribution" that lies ahead for his critics and opponents.

In that same vein, it is impossible to miss the poorly-hidden fact that Donald Trump has no particular fondness for the concept of "unity" – albeit that our country's first name is, after all, "United!" And as this cartoon also points out – Trump's "big lie" notwithstanding – the actual data show that any envisioned retribution against Trump's adversaries would necessarily be taken on behalf of a minority of voters against the much larger majority in the 2020 election. That's a number of in excess of 7,000,000 more votes than those for whom Trump evidently has his "retribution" in mind on his smaller minority "base's" behalf.

Finally, in connection with the point of this cartoon, the title of a popular song by Pink comes to mind: "What about us?"

Published by Cartoon Arts International, 3/15/2023

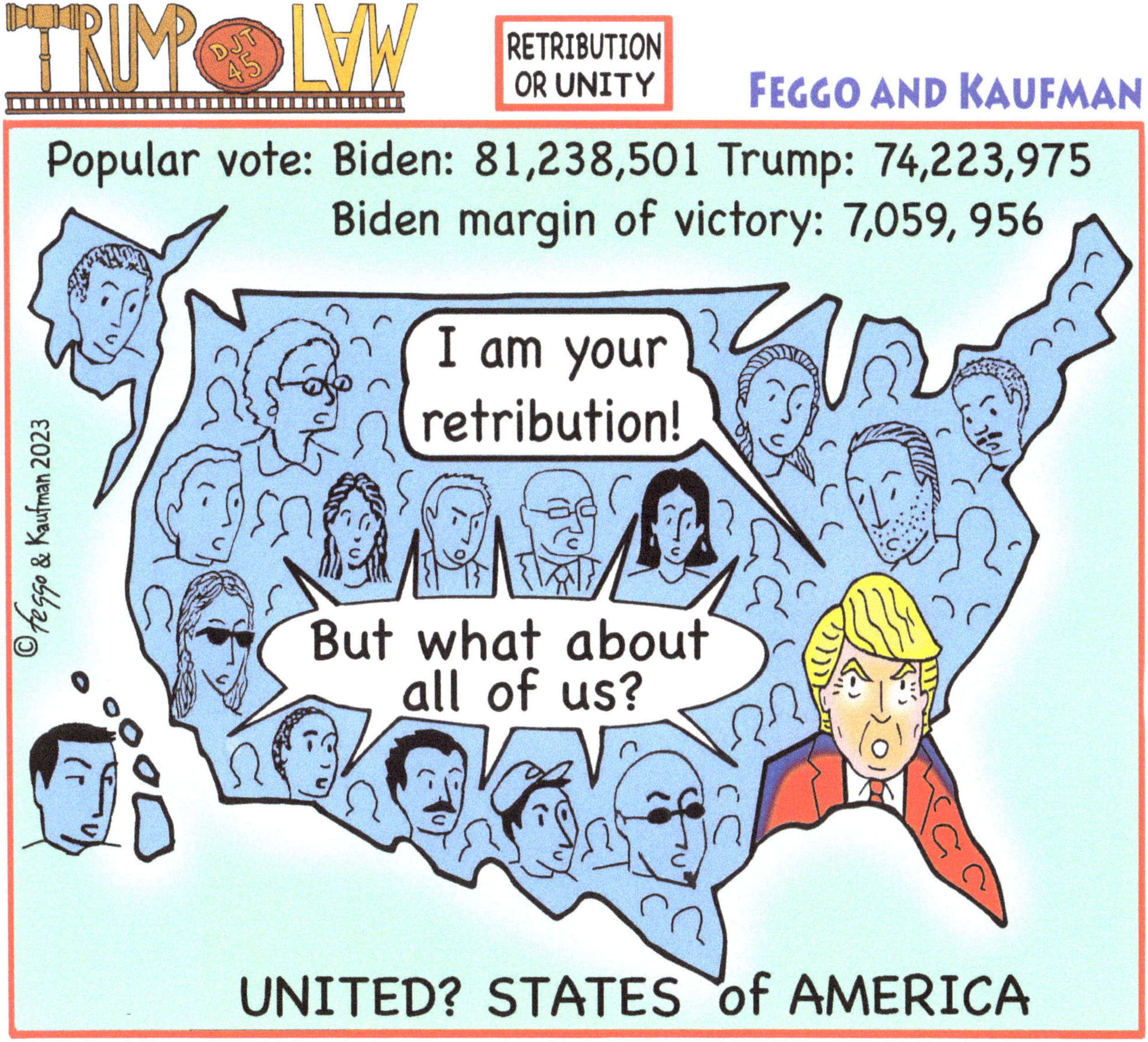

# FEGGO AND KAUFMAN

Perry and Mason are quickly back, still speaking of Trump's plans for "retribution!" But this time Perry is quick to make a lawyer's point that "retribution" is actually a legal term of art. And so Trump's retributive plans also actually represent a serious departure – as Trump is so wont to do – from governance under the "rule of law." As it turns out, however, in this cartoon Trump gets a break whether he appreciates it or not. It's too early – at least in the logic of comic books – for Trump to be deposited in the volcanic inferno. As readers will see, there will be time for that later on!

Published by Cartoon Arts International, 3/17/2023

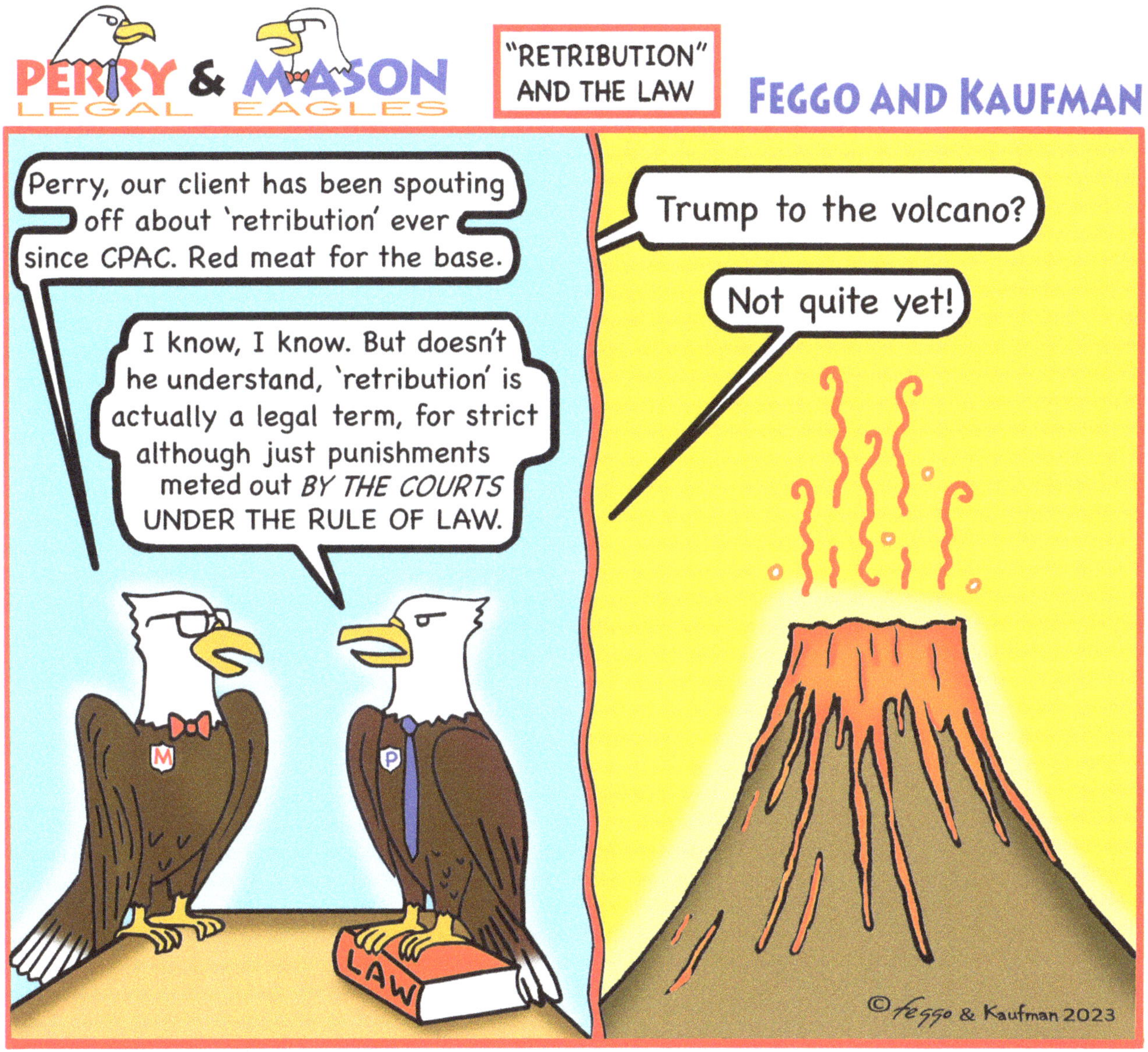

"RETRIBUTION" AND THE LAW

FEGGO AND KAUFMAN

Still in his early, hyper-aggressive stage in relation to the legal charges being pursued against him, readers may recall that Donald Trump warned of potential "death & destruction" if he faced criminal charges in New York County state court in connection with his alleged, so-called "hush-money" payments to porn star "Stormy Daniels." In this cartoon, Trump is already self-consciously preparing for his first "perp walk" in New York City. (See also "Wheels of Justice" cartoon, infra.) Finally, readers may also recall that a similarly aggressive reaction by Trump was provoked by federal execution of a search warrant (in the period August/September 2022) for unreturned classified documents that Trump was still mystifyingly hoarding at Mar-A-Lago.

Published by Cartoon Arts International, 3/24/2023

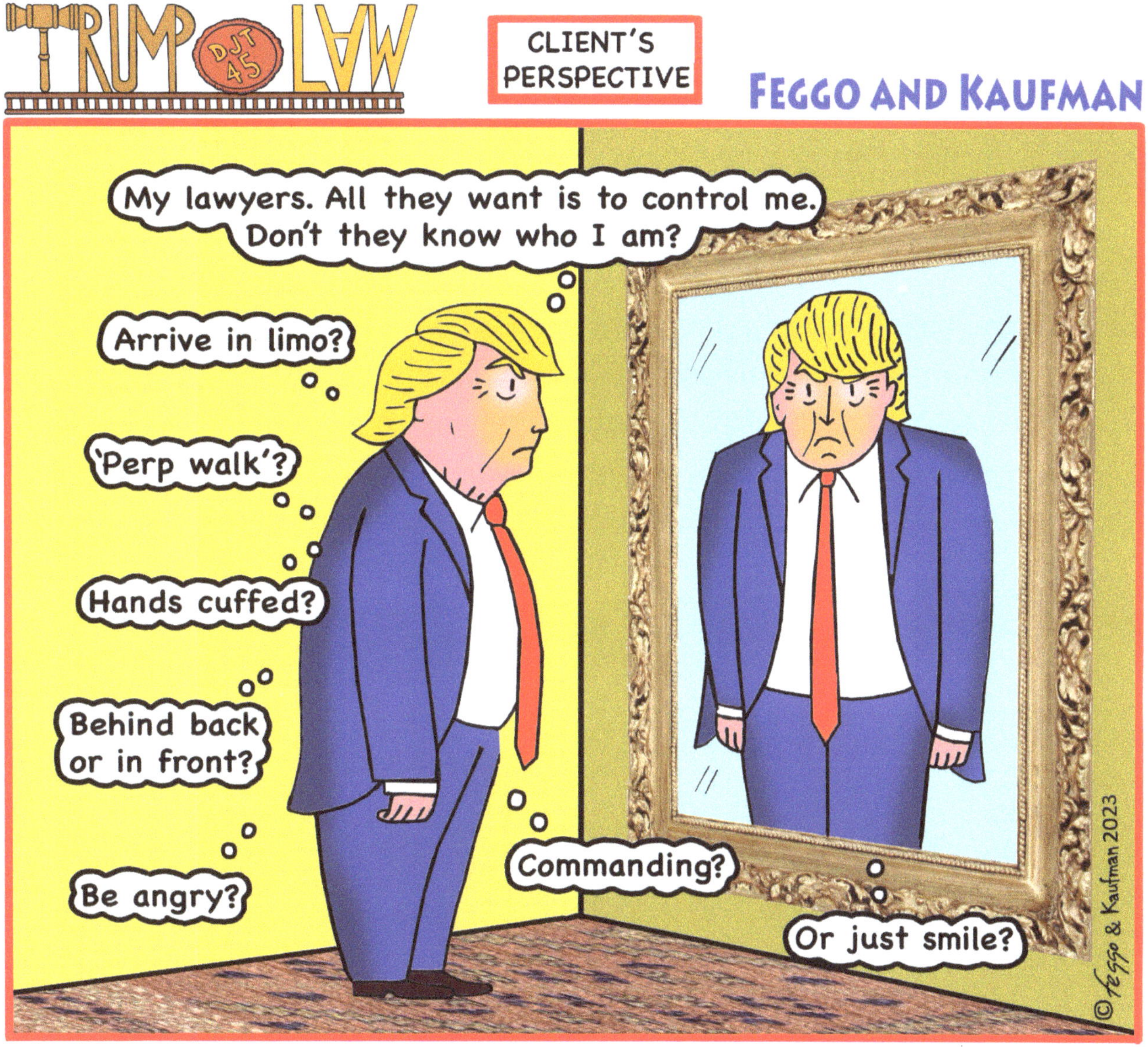

CLIENT'S PERSPECTIVE

# FEGGO AND KAUFMAN

For his "Legal Eagle" attorneys, Perry and Mason, Trump's intransigence would again lead to serious, albeit unabashedly cartoonish, threats of bodily injury to Trump if he were to have been dropped by his feathered counsel into the cauldron of an active volcano over which he again found himself being dangled. Of course, this is still relatively early on in Trump's political and legal campaign to be reinstated to the Oval Office in 2024. And at this preliminary point in time, "control of the client" was more of a dream and far less of a reality for Perry and Mason.

Published by Cartoon Arts International, 3/24/2023; also published @DavidCayJ, 3/22/23

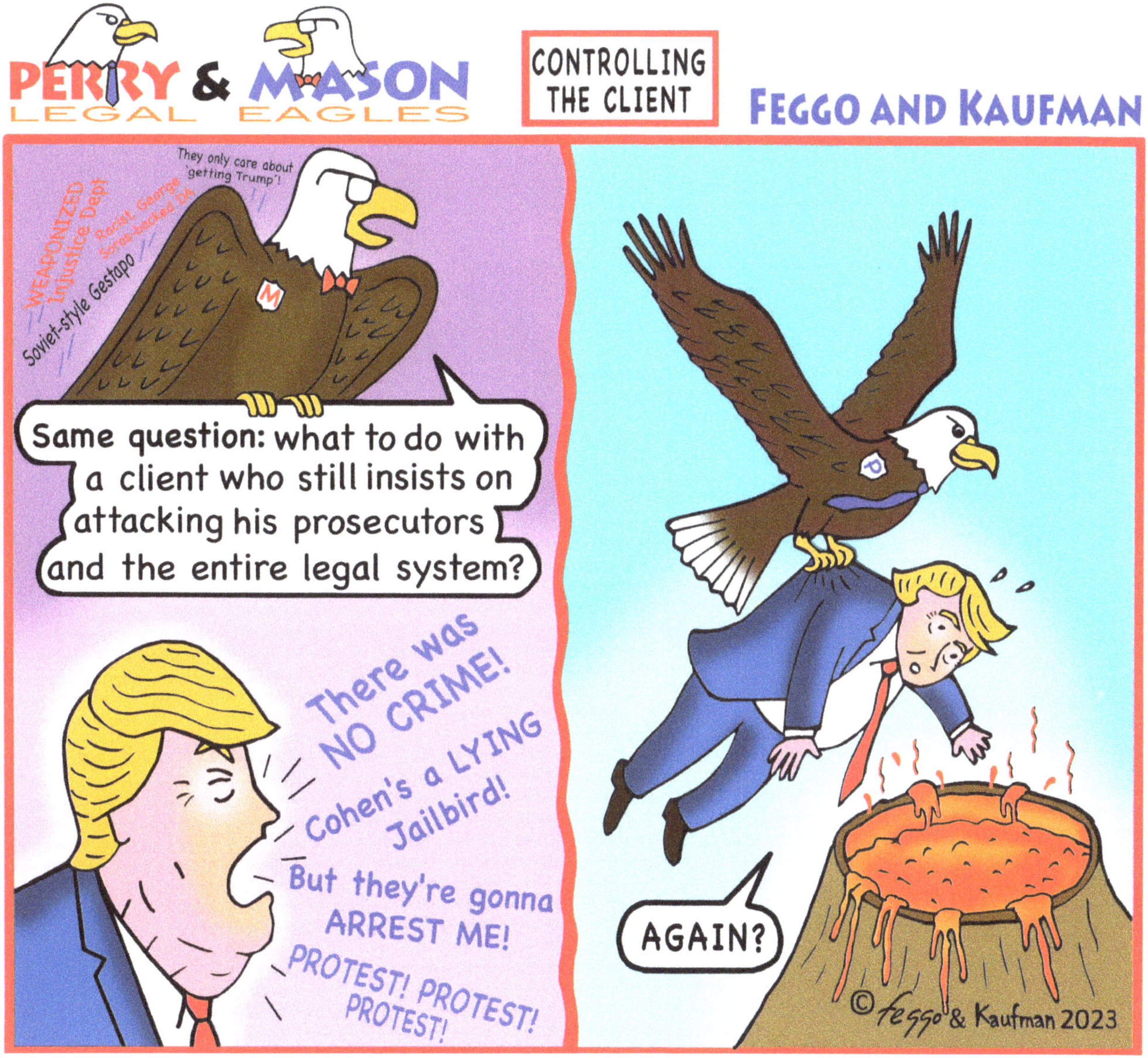

# PERRY & MASON — LEGAL EAGLES



# FEGGO AND KAUFMAN

In this cartoon, here is Donald Trump at his most officious, dramatically asserting a claimed prerogative to make controlling decisions about the legal or historical adequacy of the many legal charges being asserted against him. If you look closely at the setting of the cartoon you will see that the apparent presidential desk – overloaded with largely-ignored complaints of one kind or another – is actually not in the White House but is part some kind of a phony stage set ironically located in an insecure storage area at Mar-a-Lago. In fact, in the background can be seen a small stack of what appear to be some of the many "boxes" of presidential documents that should long ago have been returned to the government upon its request. And so the control Trump appears to be asserting over the various complaints being made against him (organized in trays on his desk) is only that: i.e., apparent but not actual control of the situation and its national security concerns.

Published by Cartoon Arts International, 3/30/2023

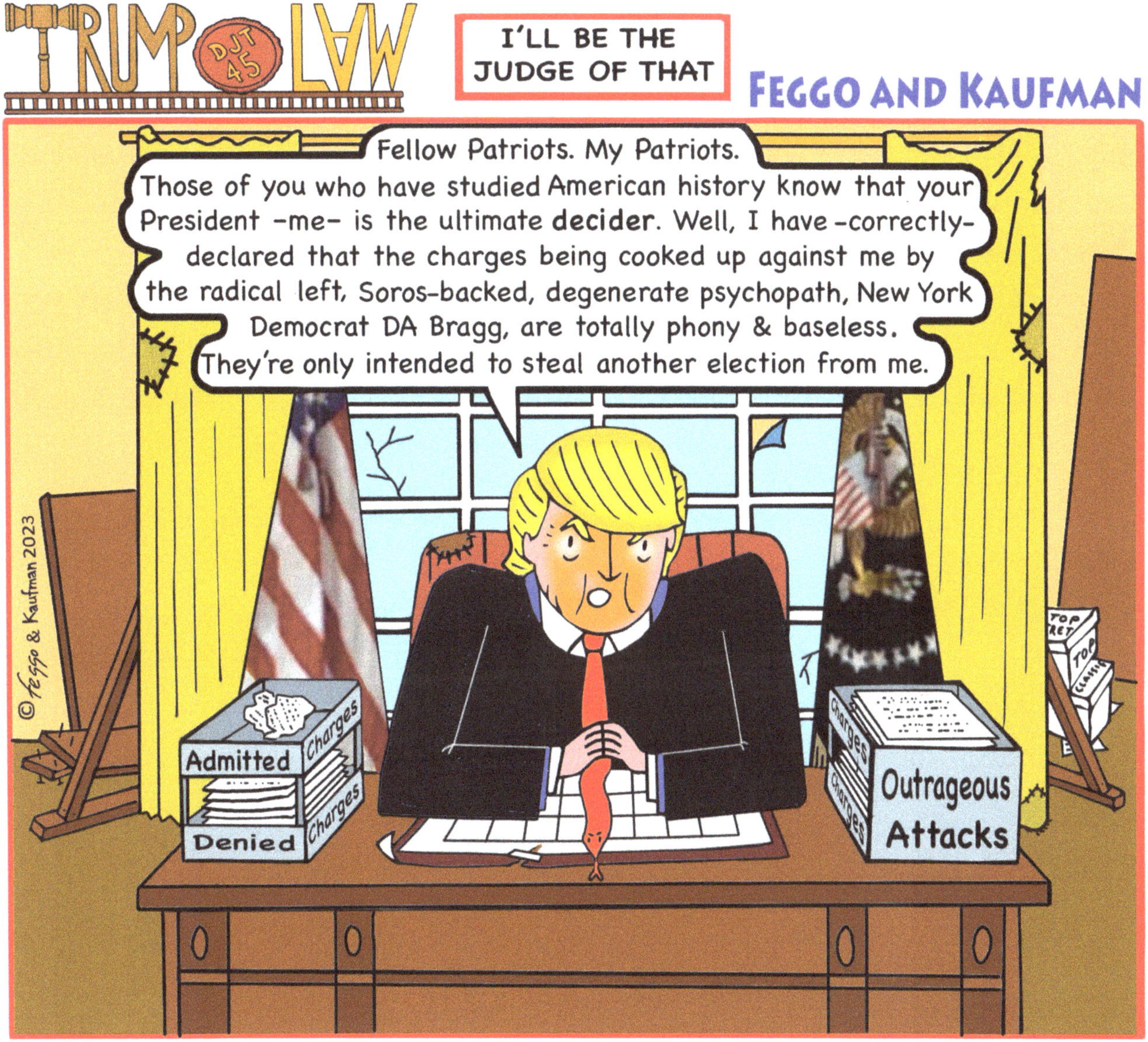

I'LL BE THE JUDGE OF THAT

# FEGGO AND KAUFMAN

In this cartoon, Trump's Legal Eagles have returned, still complaining about their client's failure to follow sound legal advice. The two sides represented by the ongoing conflict between attorneys Perry and Mason, on the one hand, and their client on the other, is now matched in the two signs held by picketers in front of the New York County Criminal Courthouse. In this rendition of the Trumpian world, we have yet another divide between between the MAGA (or WWG1WGA) crowd and the opposite crowd relieved to see Donald Trump – "finally!" (or at least possibly?) – being brought to justice – this time in the New York Criminal Court.

Of course, although this cartoon was originally published more than a year ago (4/4/23) we find ourselves now still awaiting the commencement of Trump's trial as of the middle of April of the following year (2024). Yet still, as close followers know, a first trial that could be finished by spring or early summer, puts this case well ahead of the several other cases languishing – for one reason or another – in one or another court at the present time – up to and including the Supreme Court of the United States.

Published by Cartoon Arts International, 4/4/2023

We told him not to constantly attack his prosecutors.
NY CRIMINAL COURT
WWG1 WGA!
MAGA
MAGA
45
FINALLY!
© Feggo & Kaufman 2023

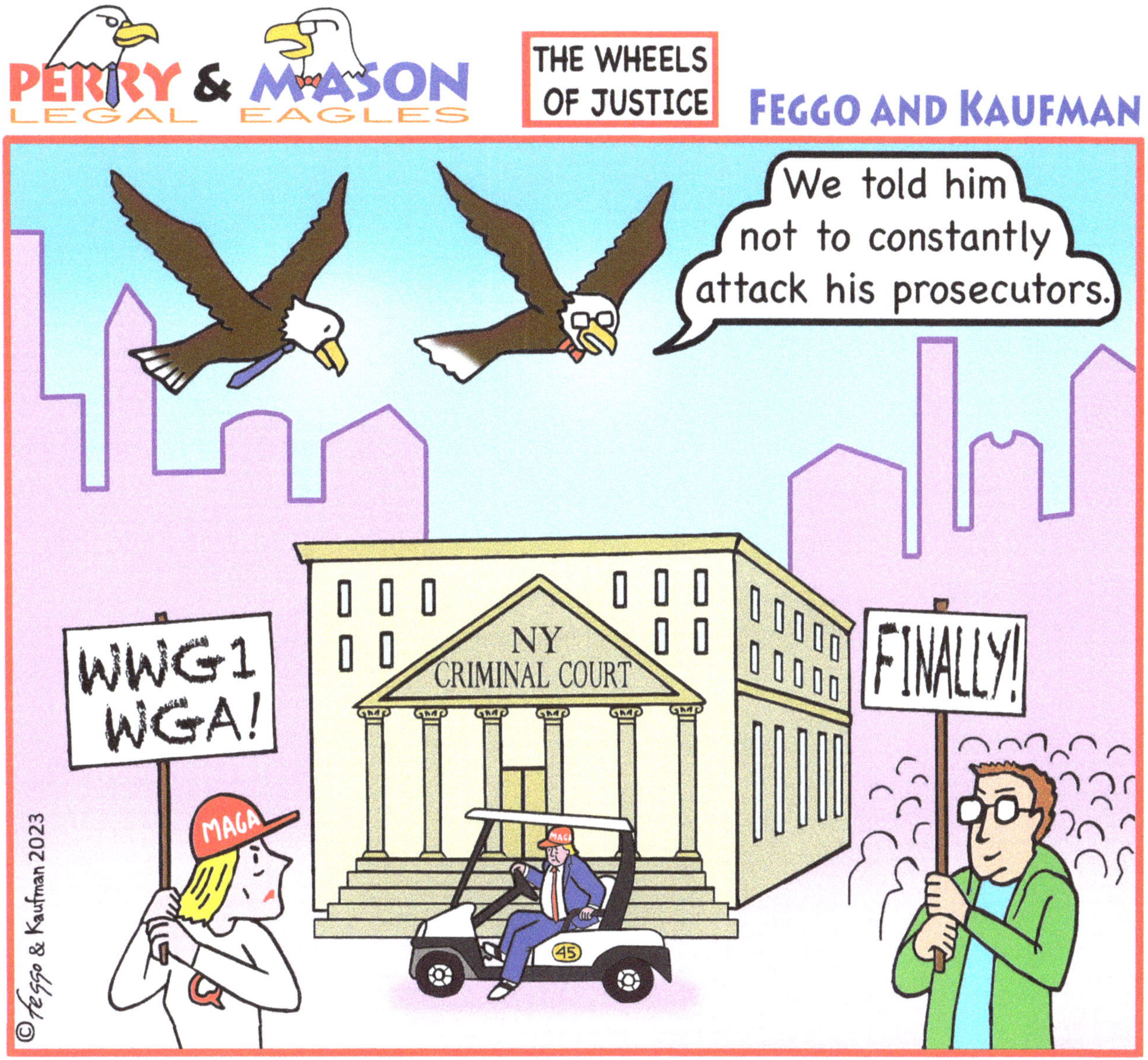

In this cartoon Trump is once again showing his true colors under pressure from a judge
in one of his cases, to control his outrageous attacks on prosecutors, witnesses and the
judicial system. As is shown, Trump's pretense of remorse (on the left) is immediately
followed by contemptuous attacks (on the right) – reproduced essentially verbatim – that
are still going on to this day more than a year later. With many "gag orders" entered,
but with none yet fully complied with. It may finally be time – soon? – for Trump's
outrageous behavior to be brought under control. However, readers are advised –
certainly – not to hold their individual or collective breathes for this to occur.


Published by Cartoon Arts International, 4/6/2023

# TRUMP LAW





## FEGGO AND KAUFMAN

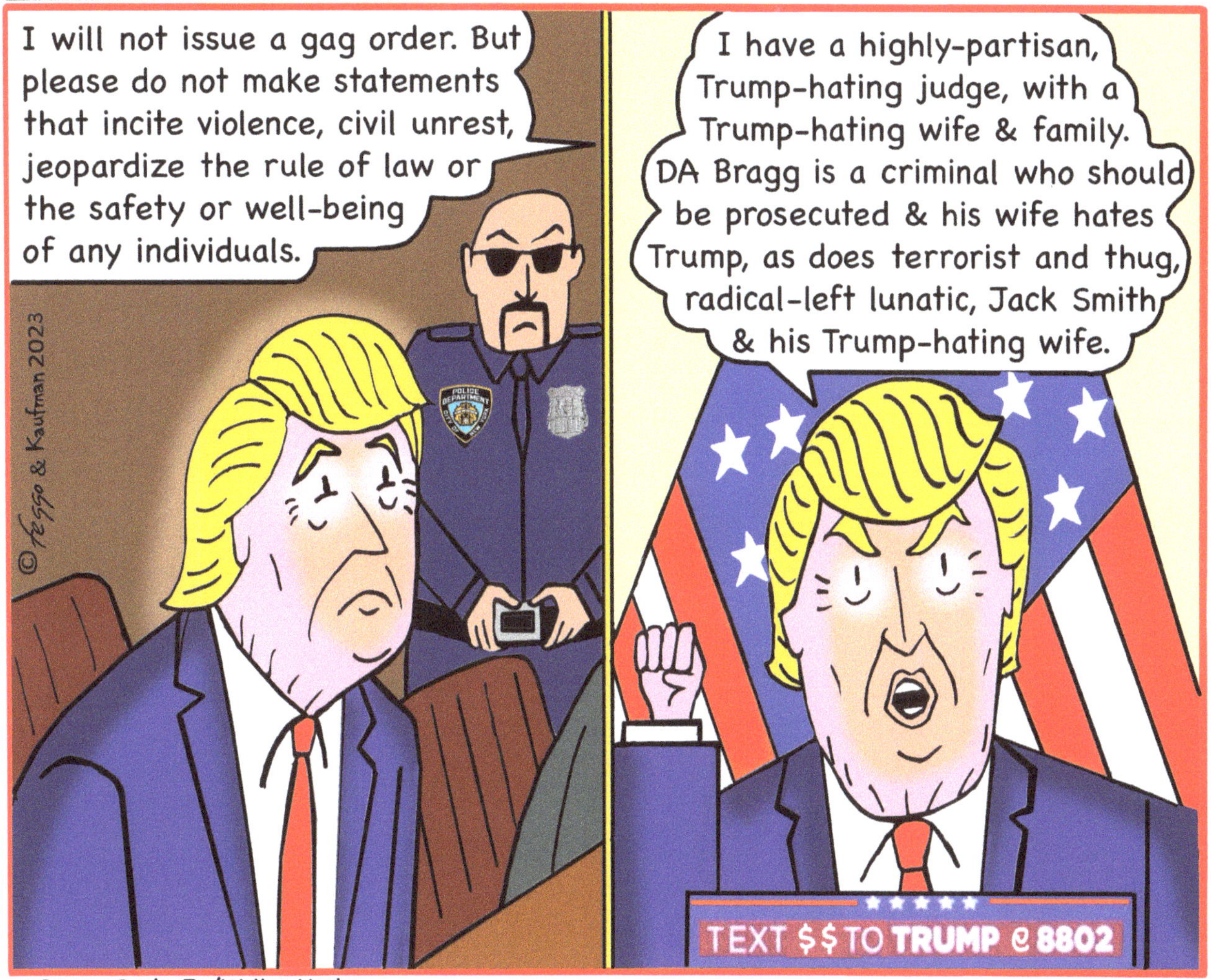

* Sammy Davis, Jr./Walter Marks

In this cartoon we find ourselves reflecting on Trump's constant and continuing admiration for "strongmen" around the world – men uninterested in compliance with the rule [of] law. Of course, Vladimir Putin continues to be the strong man of strongmen as depicted in several of the cartoons in this and our earlier book. Perhaps one day of the world will know the full explanation for the power and consistency of Putin's hold over Trump. Or, for that matter, maybe never! Victor Orban of Hungary is now another chosen flavor of the month dictator, so to speak. Life imitating art, Orban having actually been invited to the United States by his kind of Republicans in Congress and/or by the defeated former president himself. And in the era of Trump, there is evidently no shame or reluctance to be seen hobnobbing with any one of Trump's favorite dictators!

Published by Cartoon Arts International, 4/15/2023

TRUMP DJT 45 LAW
RULE OF WITHOUT LAW
FEGGO AND KAUFMAN
PRIVATE ROOM DO NOT ENTER!
Heroes, each one of them! A great country needs a strong man!
Feggo & Kaufman 2023

This cartoon, titled "Defamation," gives us a speedy yet almost comprehensive tour of some of the freakish events surrounding the defamation issue in the world of Donald Trump. As one of the originators of the "big lie" of a stolen election – up to and including allegations of "rigged" voting machines – Trump's fantasy of a lawsuit by him against Fox is not entirely beyond imagining, considering Fox's headline-making, three-quarters of a billion-dollar defamation settlement with Dominion Voting Systems. Of course, the Legal Eagles already sense that such a claim by Donald Trump might well not be one worth betting on in terms of perhaps a contingent fee arrangement in lieu of "cash up front."

Published by Cartoon Arts International, 4/21/2023

PERRY & MASON
LEGAL EAGLES
DEFAMATION
FEGGO AND KAUFMAN



Now Trump wants to sue Fox for defamation!
How so?
Trump claims Fox's giant settlement with Dominion implies he lied about the stolen 2020 election!
If he wants us to take that case, it's gotta be cash up front.
He offered us Series 2 of his Digital Trading Cards! He says Series 1 already sold out!
Once a grifter, always a grifter!
DOMINION
FOX NEWS
SETTLEMENT
© Feggo & Kaufman 2023

We now arrive at the first of the multiplicity of legal claims against Donald Trump still pending, in one fashion or another, to the date of this publication. Here, we deal with E. Jean Carroll whose defamation claims against the defeated former President ultimately cost him just shy of $100,000,000 – subject of course to the possibility of reversal or reduction on appeal. In this cartoon, Trump is forgetting that, during a trip to one of his golf courses in Scotland, he led the press to believe that he would definitely travel  back to New York to testify at "Miss Bergdorf Goodman's" defamation action against him. Surprise, surprise – this promise turned out to be yet another baseless lie. I'd like to say it ain't so. But I can't. In Trump's life golf – and lying – often do take precedence over what he deems to be less important matters such as truth and propriety and application of the rule of law!


Published by Cartoon Arts International, 4/29/2023.

TRUMP DJT 45 LAW
DEFENDING IN ABSENTIA
FEGGO AND KAUFMAN
He raped me... Whether I screamed or not... I was fighting... Those are the facts.
JUDGE L. KAPLAN
D. J. TRUMP
E. JEAN CARROLL
©feggo & Kaufman 2023
She is not my type. Miss Bergdorf Goodman case. You can grab them by the... A made up SCAM! Fraudulent and false. A witch hunt.
MAGA
1-6

This cartoon represents an early, rapid-pace summation of Trump's multiplicity of legal woes. With Trumpian defense strategies already lined up for each one of them. Needless to say, they are "witch hunts" all! A "perfect" call to Georgia. Carroll's not my type. A Trump-hating judge. A racist prosecutor. And those boxes: Biden had more, don't you know?

Published by Cartoon Arts International, 5/4/2023

# TRUMP LAW

## DEFENSE STRATEGIES

## FEGGO AND KAUFMAN

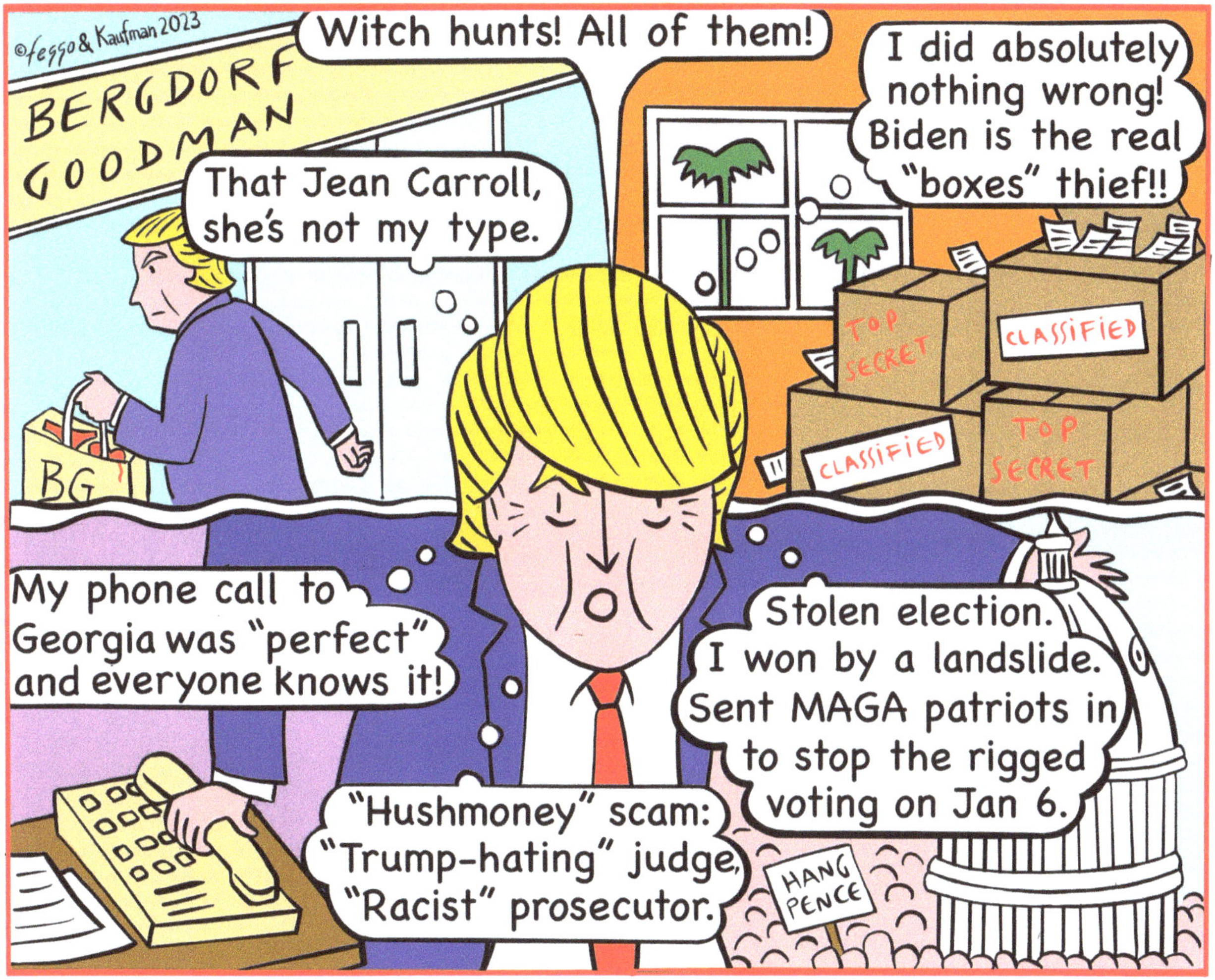

This (pre)historic cartoon is based on one of those uber-memorable snippets from Trump testimony that, it seems, can always be found in one transcript or another, generated in one case or another. Here, famously, Trump was asked (at a deposition in the E. Jean Carroll sexual assault case, in October 2022) whether he considered himself to be a "star" who could "get away" with grabbing any woman by the genitalia. (DJT: "I guess you could say that.") Trump then went on to offer a quick summary of "the last million years" of world history: "for better or worse, if you're a star, historically that's true – fortunately or unfortunately." And so, in this cartoon, we simply run with one of Trump's many deposition bloopers.

Published on Twitter, @henry_kaufman20, 5/8/23

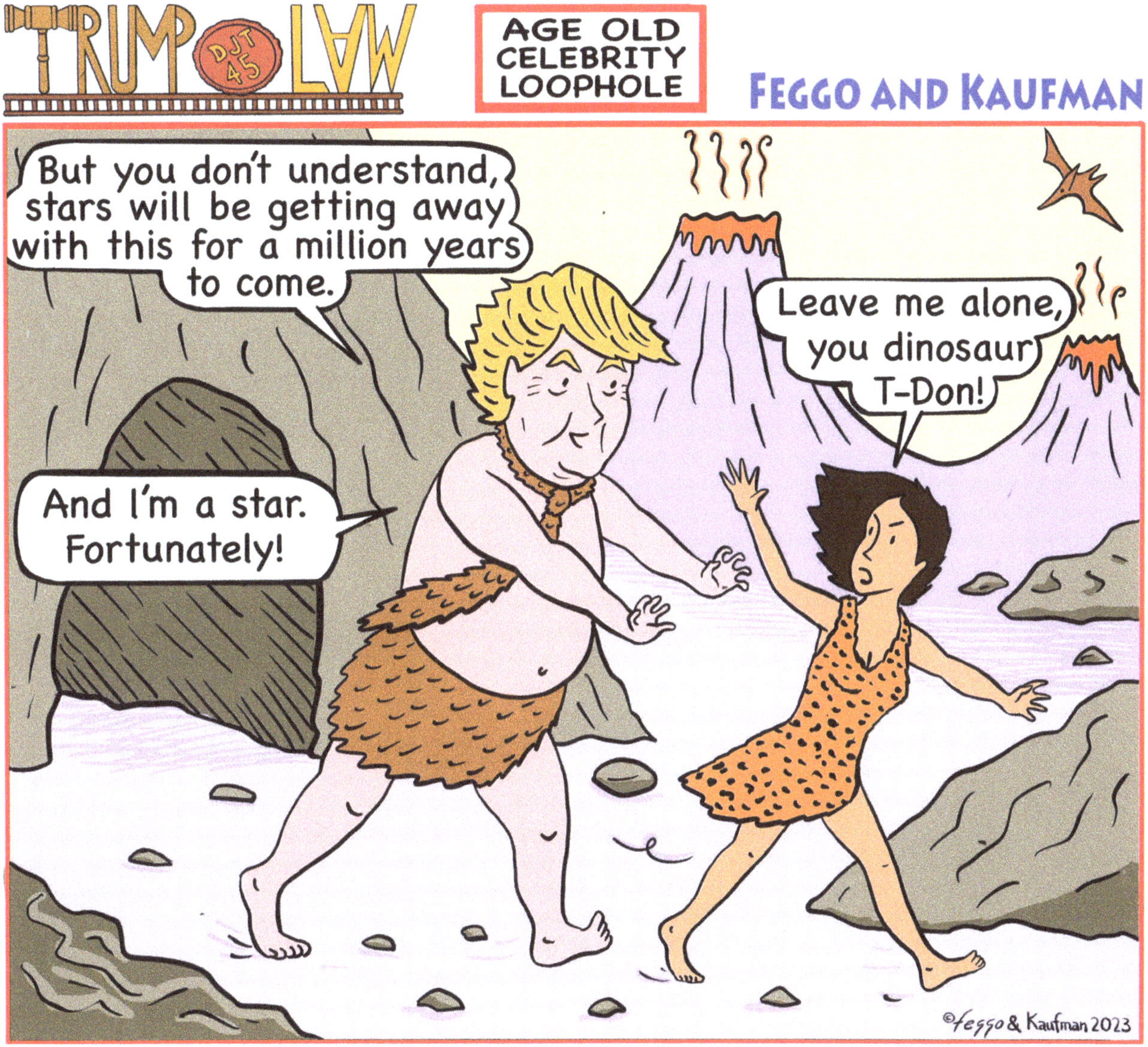

# FEGGO AND KAUFMAN

Observing Donald Trump for even a brief period of time can drive one to a very cynical conclusion. He's not very bright and does not know how to leave well enough alone; if he wants to say something, he will say something. And if he wants to repeat something he will do that too. Whether or not it gets him into more trouble – as here, where he repeats a defamation that had already led to a very substantial 7-figure jury verdict awarded against him earlier that very same week.

Still, here we find Trump participating in a nationally-broadcast "Town Hall." And what does he do? He repeats the very same position that had already been held defamatory and subject to a seven-figure damage award. But even after this cartoon, Trump continued to repeat the defamation, time and again. And so, after a separate damages trial, the awards against him in the E. Jean Carroll case had risen dramatically to the high eight-figures (more than $83,000,000)!

Published on Twitter @henry_kaufman20, 5/12/23

PERRY & MASON
LEGAL EAGLES
RE-DEFAMATION TRUMP STYLE
FEGGO AND KAUFMAN



Perry, didn't we tell Trump to stop calling people names?
Yeah. But then he defamed 'Miss Bergdorf Goodman' a second time.
And now he owes her $5 million!
Well he did it all over again at the CNN 'Town Hall.' Called Carroll a 'whack job' pushing a 'fake story'. Claimed the 'Clinton-appointed' judge hates him. And that the New York City jury was 'partisan' and 'anti-trump.'
I rest my case!
© Feggo & Kaufman 2023

Donald Trump is seen here in an unusual position. As opposed to most of our Trump cartoons, Trump is actually lying down instead of being in constant motion. There are apparently two related reasons for this: Trump is in fact rarely ever seen lying down but is almost always seen on the move in one fashion or another. In addition, we believe we know, from many reports, that Trump is not a book reader. Here however, for some reason, Donald Trump is reading a lawbook – of all things – apparently boning up on the law of Georgia. In his copy of the standard resource, Black's Law Dictionary (misspelled in the cartoon – sorry about that) he is being schooled in the absurdity of his claims of "perfect" phone calls for purposes of resolving legal disputes. Indeed, in what may perhaps be unique in all of Black's Law Dictionary, that otherwise generally neutral legal text – somehow, with pointed and biting satire – specifically directed at Trump's pretentious claim to "perfection." I don't know. Do you think that might be something of an interpolation by the authors of this book? Here putting their hands on the scale of neutrality? And that perhaps you will not find the entirety of this definition – undermining Trump's ridiculous claims – in Black's Law Dictionary itself??

Published @henry_kaufman20, 5/15/23

TRUMP LAW
DJT 45
GEORGIA ON MY MIND*
FEGGO AND KAUFMAN
That racist prosecutor in Atlanta is about to indict me for a PERFECT phone call!
BLACK LAW'S DICTIONARY
GA
Perfect: Only the judge or jury may decide if alleged acts by the defendant are lawful or unlawful. A claim of "perfection" by the accused is irrelevant. It is also ridiculous.
© Feggo & Kaufman 2023
*Hoagy Carmichael

From its inception, I have loved the simplicity of this cartoon. Yet its seeming simplicity belies the complex conclusions that stand behind them – at least in terms of the competing investigations that underlie each of the two "poker" hands. Essentially, the hand on the right, held by the woman on whose white sash is written a single word, "TRUTH," loosely stands for the result of the monumental investigation led by Special Counsel Robert Mueller, producing two substantial, published volumes. However, one of the Legal Eagles is flying Mueller away from the poker game. The other hand is held by Donald Trump, symbolizing the so-called Durham report, ordered and produced by Republicans in order to provide what have become known in the Trump era as "alternative facts!" And you will see that – at the same time – Durham is being flown in to the poker game, presumably to contest the Mueller investigation's findings, at least to some arguably "winning" extent.

Published @henry_kaufman20, 5/19/23

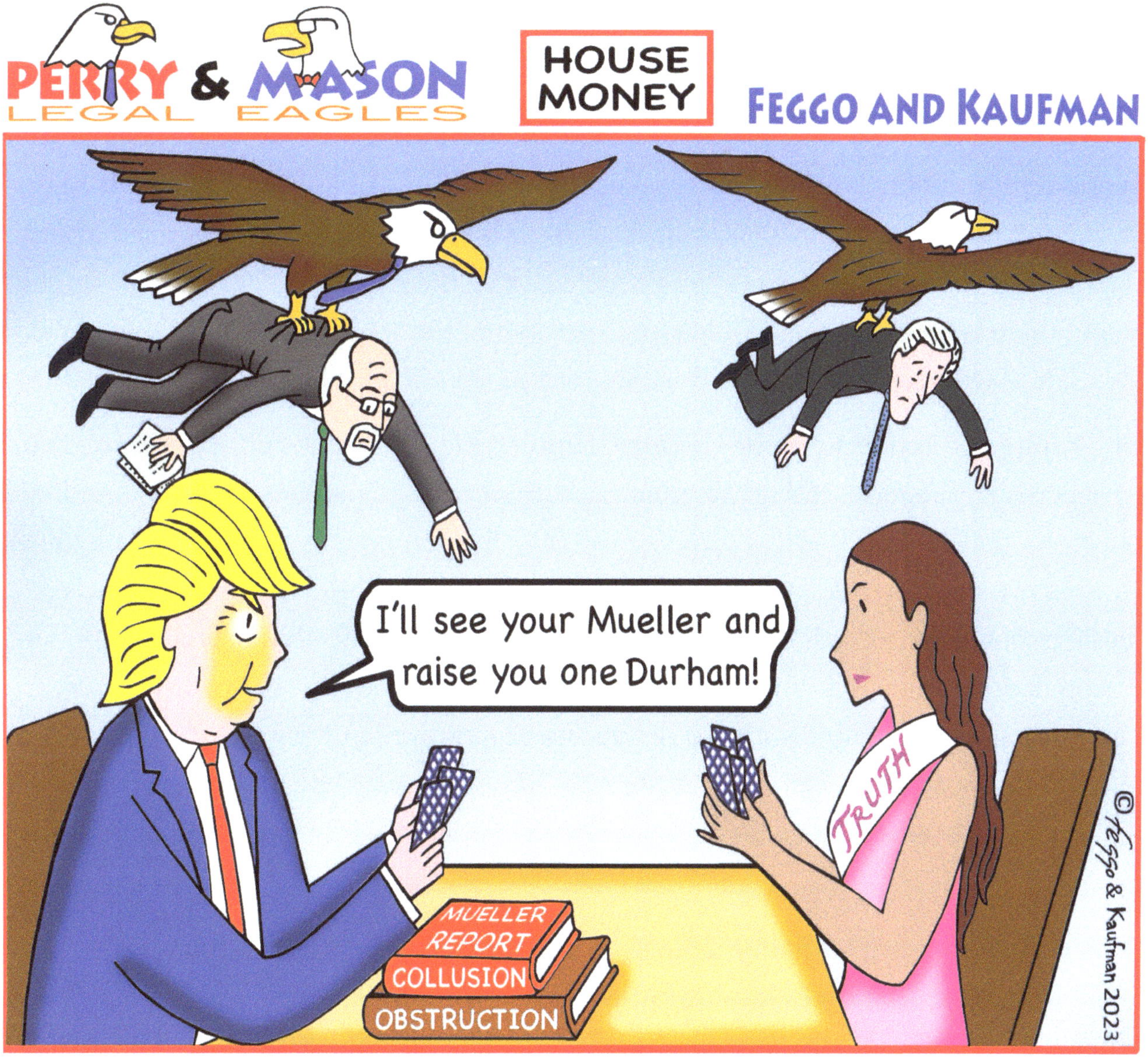

# FEGGO AND KAUFMAN

I must admit that I have never fully understood the logic of what we are calling Trump's "heroic offers" or "heroic promises" in the next four cartoons. Here is what Trump has stated to be the basic premise of his self-congratulatory heroism: "THEY'RE NOT COMING AFTER ME. I'M STANDING IN THE WAY OF THEIR COMING AFTER YOU!" By all appearances, these "heroic," and self-sacrificing sounding assurances by Trump, appear to have electrified his MAGA base, for what exact reason I find myself quite unable to explain. Perhaps it is because I am – unlike most Trump supporters – a lawyer trained in the formal ways of the American legal system. In that sense, there is no such thing as a leader "standing in the way" of anything in particular that is actually protective of his supporters as opposed to the politician himself.

For example, in connection with Trump's Heroic Offer 1, a MAGA supporter conflates his personal situation, stiffing a hometown stripper out of perhaps a couple hundred bucks, on the one hand, with Trump's $130,000 "hush money" payments, on the other, to international porn star Stormy Daniels – combined with 34 criminal counts of falsifying business records in order to cover up those payments that may also represent some kind of a federal campaign-finance violation. But no one was realistically ever going to be coming after the $200 deadbeat stripper tipper under any circumstances. And Trump was hardly standing "in the way" when he was charged with the improper payments, whereas the deadbeat tipper would almost certainly have been completely ignored by law enforcement.

In any event, I ask: how could Donald Trump have "stood in the way" – heroically or otherwise – of any such charge?

Published @henry_kaufman20, 5/27/23

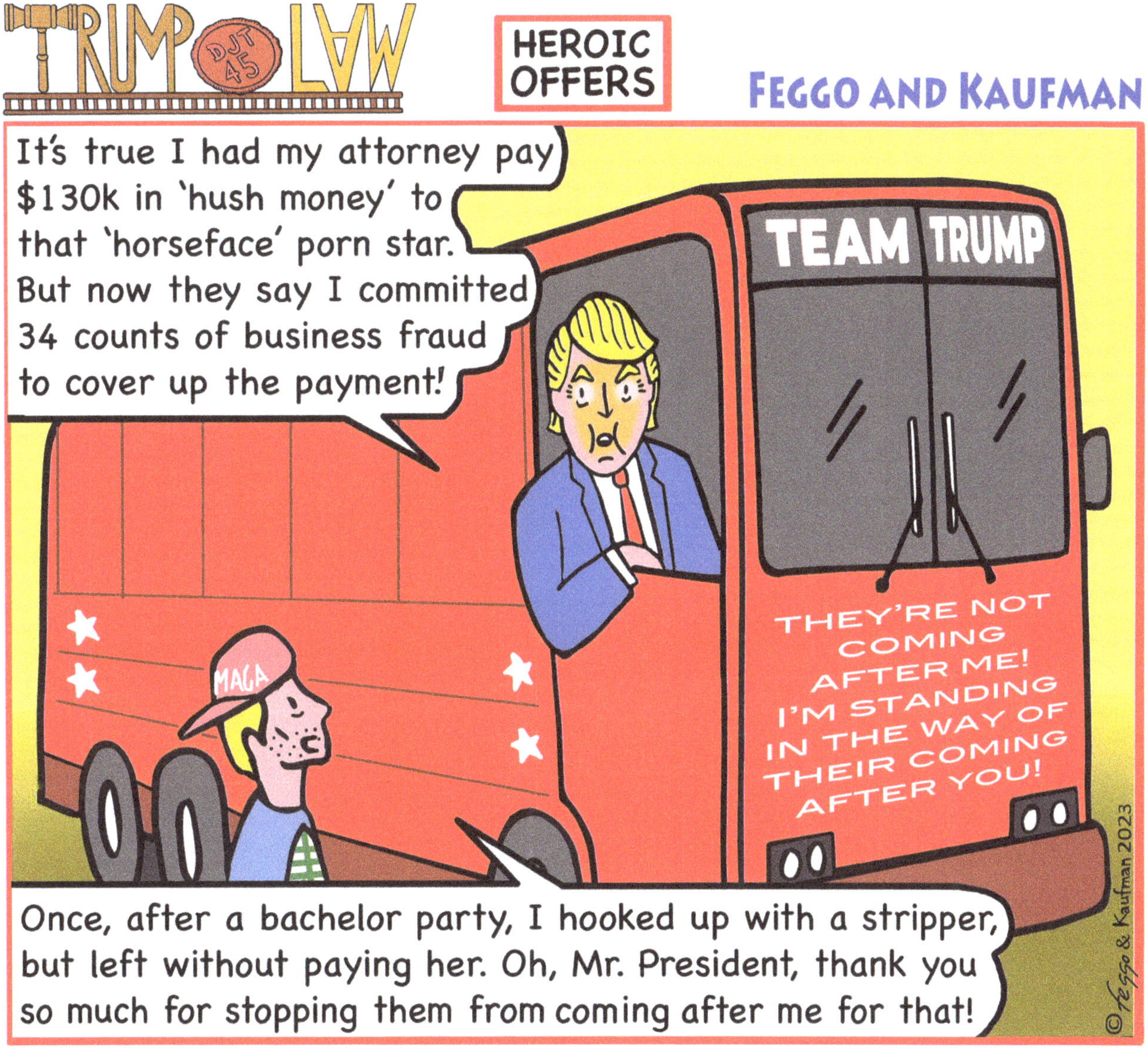

# FEGGO AND KAUFMAN

Essentially the same infirmity is inherent in Trump's "Heroic Offer 2." The Trump Organization's $5 million tax fraud – where the Company's controller Weisselberg served jail time for not reporting millions of dollars of vacation-time perks – again has absolutely nothing to do with some improper reporting – by some "John Q. Public" – of a very modest amount of betting losses at the track. Moreover, Weisselberg's $5 million fraud itself pales in comparison to the later finding of civil fraud against the Trump Organization to the tune of several hundred million dollars.

And so there is no comparison between the overreporting of modest betting losses and these millions and hundreds of millions of dollars worth of fraud attributed to the Trump Organization or its representatives. And when Donald Trump is charged with these huge fraudulent practices, he is hardly volunteering himself or his organization to take the fall in order to protect any individual fraudulently claiming minimal betting losses.

Published @henry_kaufman20, 5/30/23

## FEGGO AND KAUFMAN

And so, with apologies for the repetition, pretty much the same can be said for this third "Heroic Promise." Does anyone think it can sensibly be said that Donald Trump's inexplicable decision to stonewall his former federal government's actions to protect classified documents in his (obstinate) possession have any protective effect on the Trump loyalist's forgotten possession of overdue library books?

Published @henry_kaufman20, 6/5/23

# TRUMP LAW

## FEGGO AND KAUFMAN

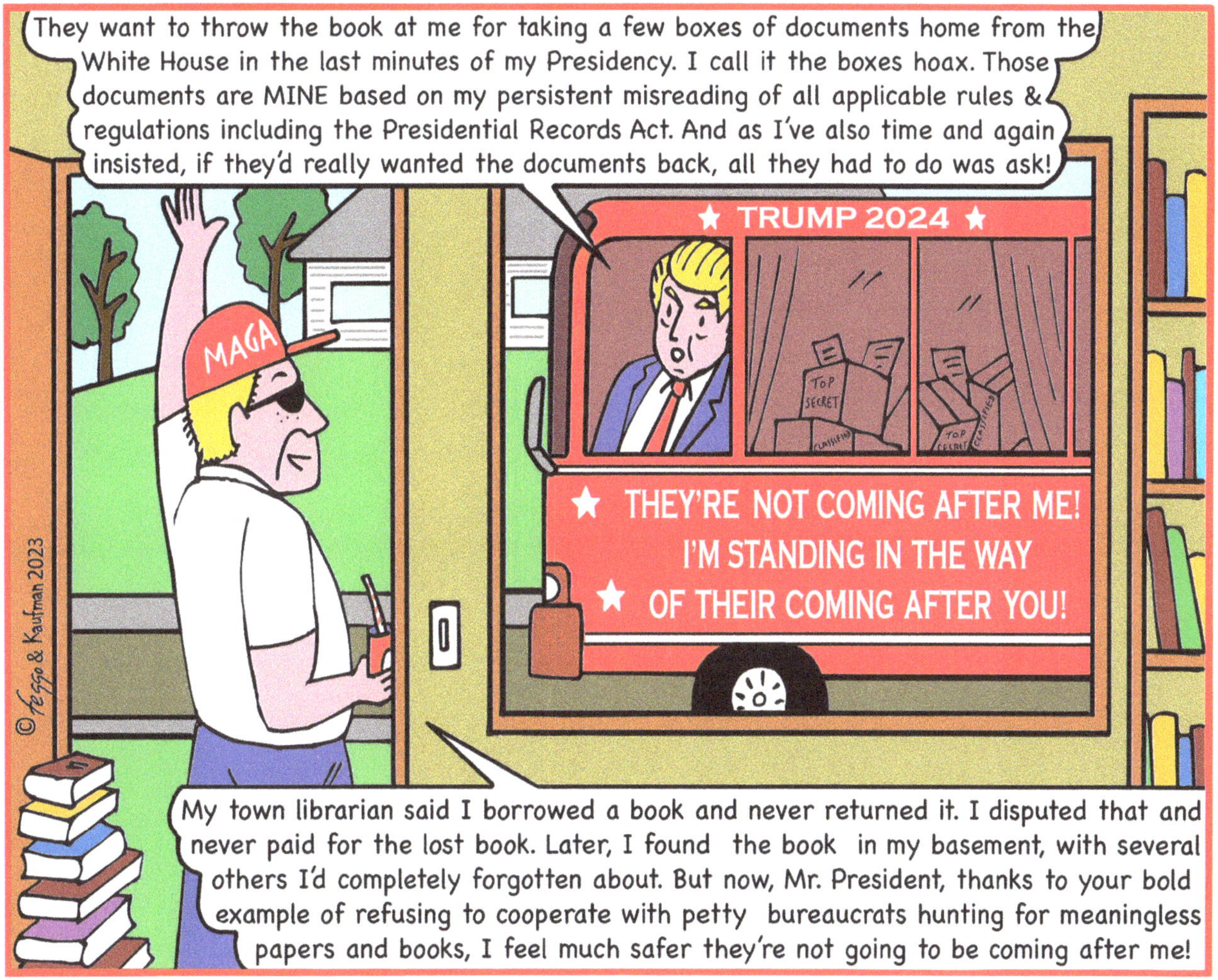

Ditto for "Heroic Promise IV." Will someone tell me how it could be that Trump's defense of his allegedly "PERFECT" phone call to Georgia's Secretary of State, could have anything in particular to do with a deep completely separate, threatening phone call by Jane Q. Citizen? Other than perhaps the implementation of a higher alert status for potentially crank calls to law enforcement – calls apparently inspired by the defeated former president.

Published @henry_kaufman20, 6/8/23

TRUMP LAW
DJT 45
HEROIC PROMISE IV
FEGGO AND KAUFMAN
© Feggo & Kaufman 2023
As I've said so many times, that racist prosecutor is trying to convict me for a "perfect" phone call! And that blabber mouth special jury forewoman basically came out and said they'd recommended me for prosecution.
WOMEN FOR TRUMP
THEY'RE NOT COMING AFTER ME ! I'M STANDING IN THE WAY OF THEIR COMING AFTER YOU!
Mr. President, inspired by your calls for patriotic action on Jan 6, I telephoned our local news station. I told them someone might get hurt if you weren't reinstated to office. Like you, I've been calling that a "perfect" phone call. I'm not sure that's working any better for me than for you in Georgia. But doesn't it make you feel that at least you're doing something to defend the indefensible?

A candid discussion and honest confession between Donald Trump and his Legal Eagle counsel. Wherein all three recognize their essences and their limitations. Does this make Trump in particular any more sympathetic or less reprehensible? That is for the citizens of America to decide! All we can do is to shine a spotlight onto the defeated former President – warts and all!!

Published on Twitter @henry_kaufman20, 6/9/23

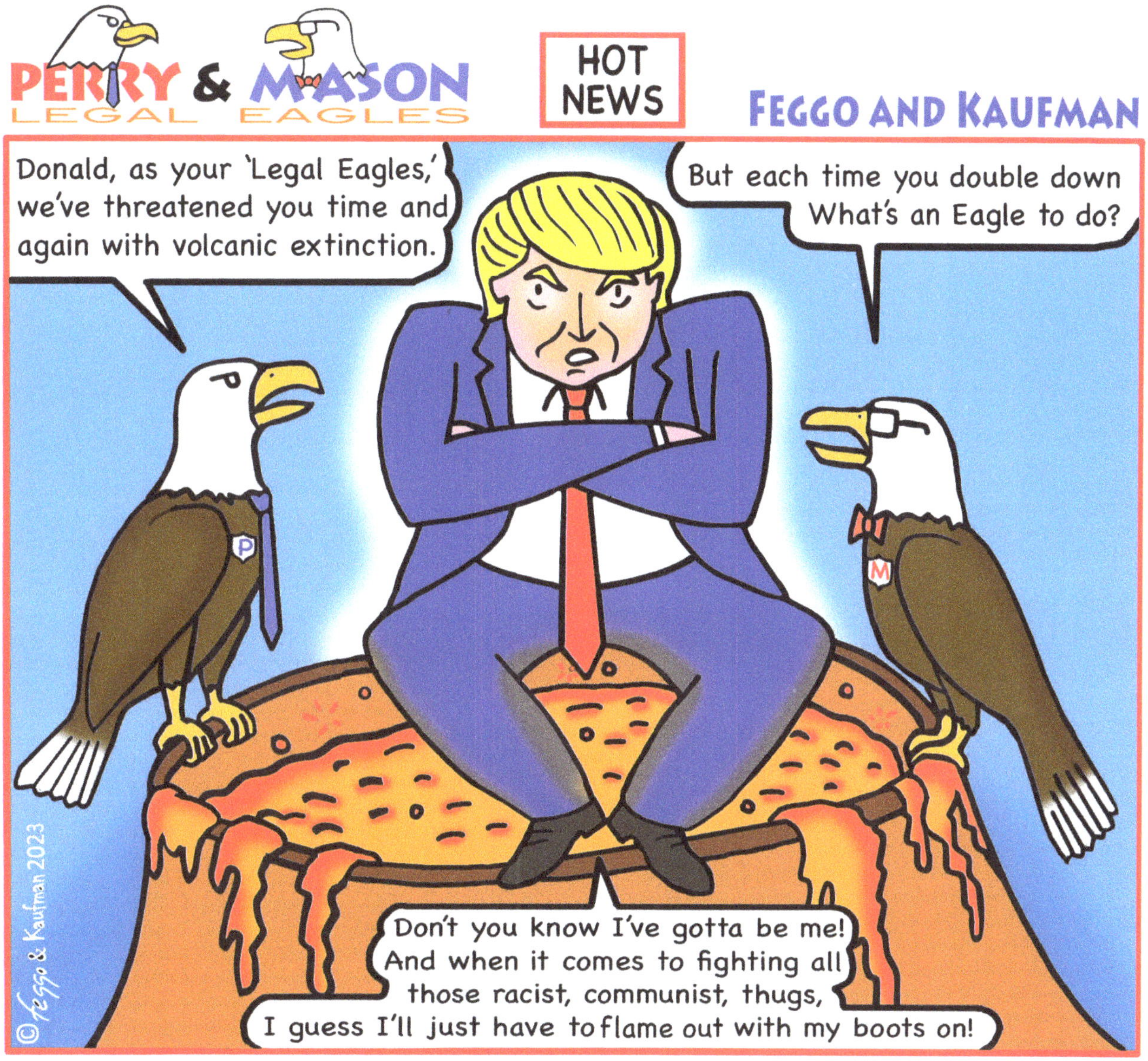

# FEGGO AND KAUFMAN

In this case, the persuasiveness of this Trumpian "heroic promise," actually no longer seems so thrilling or heroic to a Trump loyalist who – having participated in the January 6 riot – has thereafter evidently experienced the full force of federal law enforcement. Perhaps this complainant is now one of the imprisoned MAGA crowd that Trump refers to – completely brushing aside the annoying rule of law – as a "hostages." Cold comfort for those still behind bars. With their only hope being a second Trump administration's promise of pardons to Jan6 participants.

Published on Twitter @henry_kaufman20, 6/9/23

# FEGGO AND KAUFMAN

Here, Donald Trump is having the ultimate client's dream of revenge. Finally, turning
the tables on his lawyers, Perry and Mason, and holding them frighteningly over the
same boiling volcano with which the Legal Eagles have not infrequently threatened him!
You'll notice that Trump's dream is emanating from the Mar-a-Lago "boxes." And here
all Trump wants – reflecting his reality – is to have some help in making
those pesky boxes disappear!!


Published on Twitter @henry_kaufman20, 6/12/23

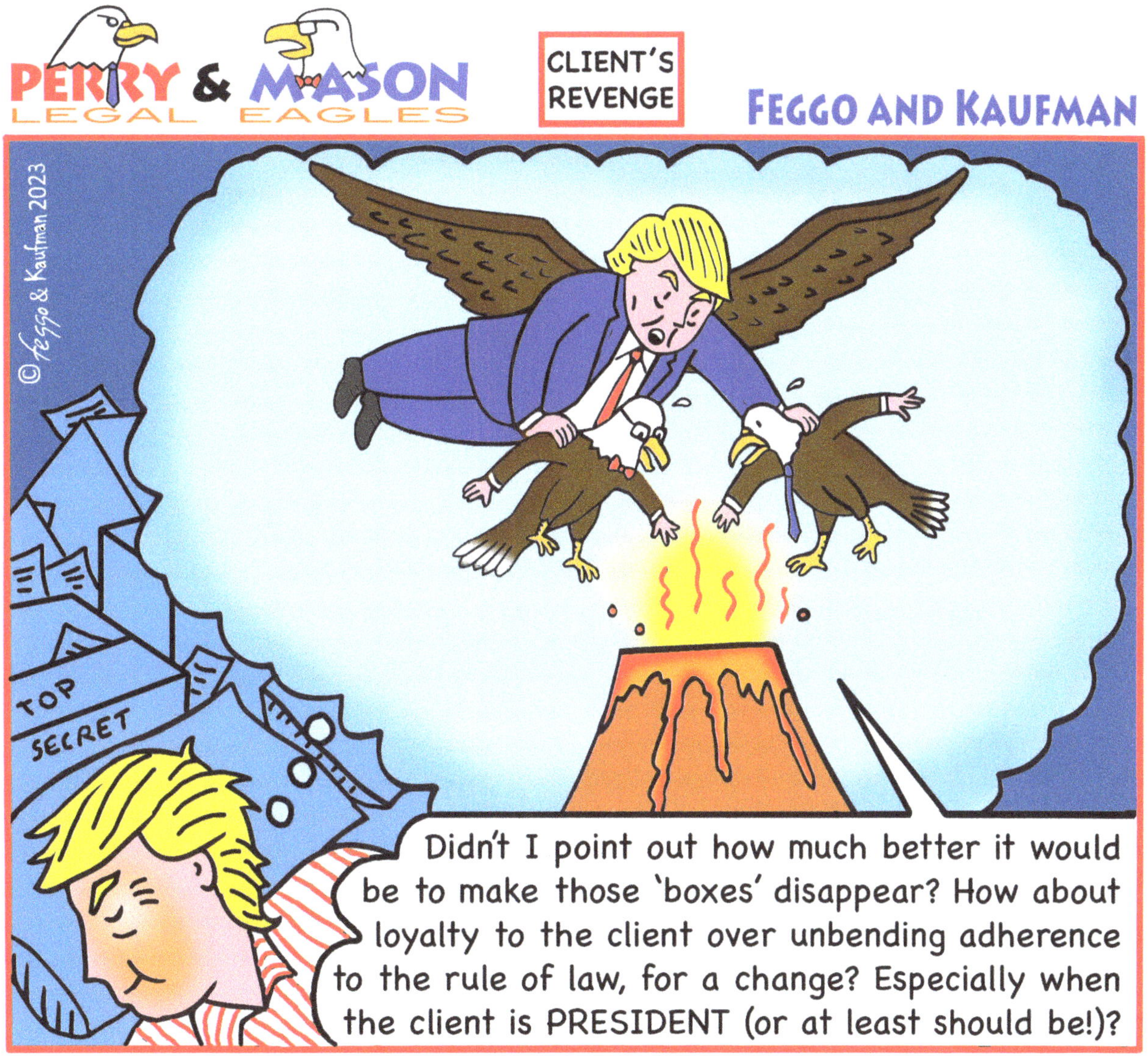

# FEGGO AND KAUFMAN

By the look of this "Summer Quarter" campus announcement board, Trump Law School/Mar-a-Lago Campus seems to be the place to be for eager law students looking to get involved in a unique set of related opportunities on a fast-track. One only hopes that the student body is not unaware of the legal issues roiling Donald Trump's Mar-a-Lago at the present time! In particular, the pending classified documents case that seems to have – wittingly or unwittingly – embroiled a number of the Mar-a-Lago executives and staff! Clearly, on this announcement board, the buyer must be aware – even as enticing as the hands-on assignments, with a great degree of responsibility, may seem to be!

Published on Twitter, @henry_kaufman20, 6/14/23

# FEGGO AND KAUFMAN

Once again we find the defeated former president taking on the mantle of a Professor at the Mar-a-Lago Law School. This time Professor Trump is attempting to articulate his take on American traditions of constitutional law. Unexpectedly for a law professor – but hardly a surprise for Donald Trump – is his focus – not on the glory or sanctity of constitutional traditions, but on how easy it is to get around them!

Published on Twitter @henry_kaufman20, 6/18/23

# TRUMP LAW

DJT 45
TRADITIONS I
FEGGO AND KAUFMAN
Welcome to ConLaw 101. I'm Professor Trump. But you can call me Mr. President.
© Feggo & Kaufman 2023
TRUMP LAW SCHOOL MAR-A-LAGO CAMPUS
Problem #1: They say we're a "constitutional democracy." Yet nothing is harder to amend than the U.S. Constitution. Trump Solution: It took until our 45th President - 45, imagine that! - to understand that the Constitution may be hard to amend, but constitutional "traditions" are easy to ignore.
Especially when you're shameless and strong - and when one-third of the country would follow you over a cliff - that means havoc can rule the day, to whatever extent required.
That's a lesson deranged Jack Smith and the Department of Injustice have yet to learn with their latest witch hunt indictment!

Here's a look at another constitutional "tradition" trampled over by the defeated 45th President and his ardent – but unthinking – supporters. That tradition is the peaceful transfer of power. Although this tradition has become obscured in the morass of other civil and criminal litigation currently involving the former President, surely the law – and the courts that enforce it – must always focus their primary attention on the overarching contest for the preservation of American democracy. For whatever Donald Trump's rationalizations may be regarding his allegedly sincere and good faith perception of a "rigged and stolen" election, it is ultimately his attempted overthrow of the principle of "the peaceful transfer of power" that "trumps" any and all other rationalizations for continuing to contest the 2020 election's outcome. There appear to be many reasons why the "rigged and stolen" claim is itself transparently baseless – indeed phony. But the overarching principle is that there must ultimately be a peaceful transition of power - and that is with or without claims of lingering concerns regarding defects in one or another aspect of the voting or vote-counting process.

Published on Twitter, @henry_kaufman20, 6/20/23

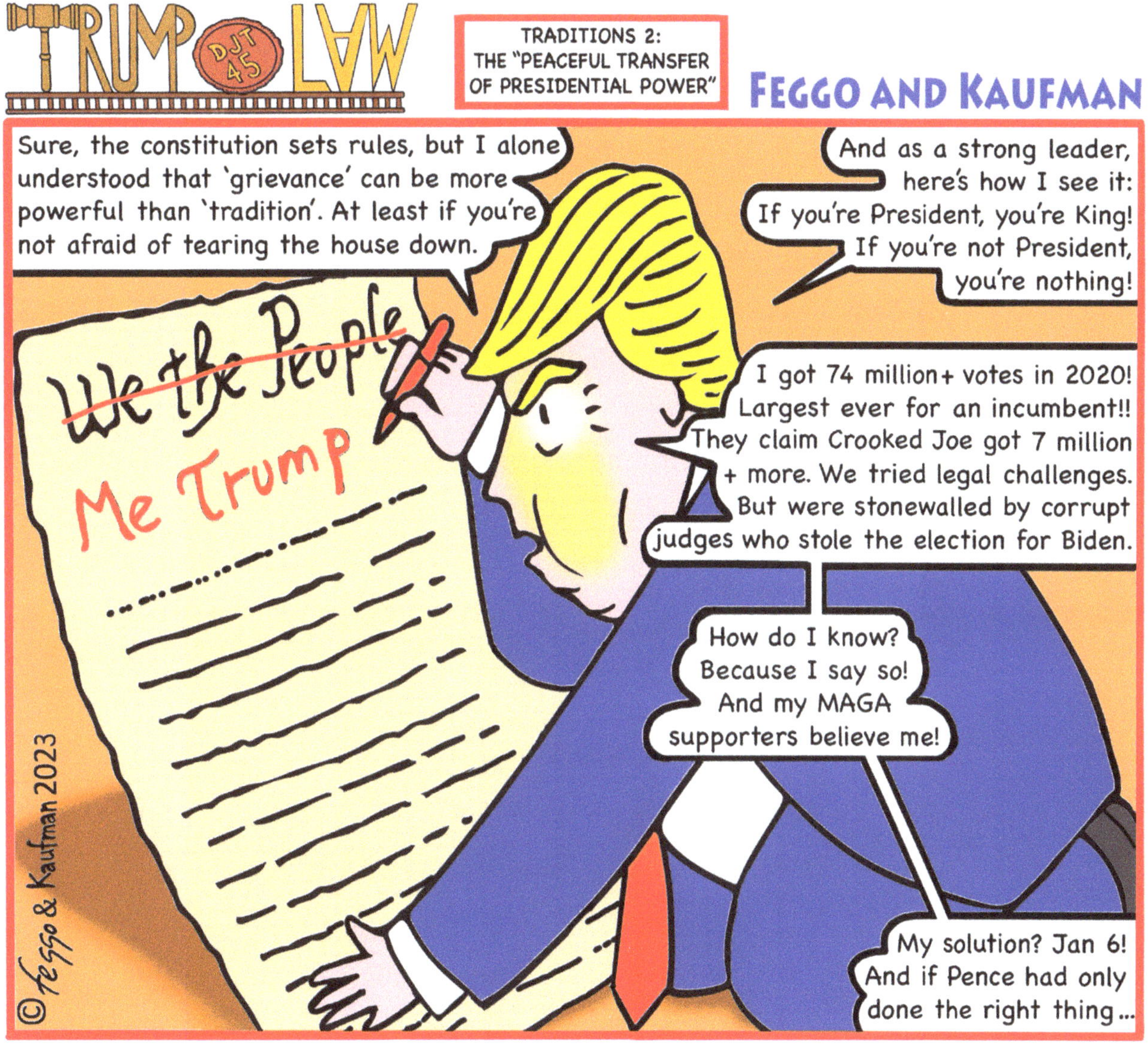

# TRUMP DJT 45 LAW

This cartoon cuts to the very essence of Donald Trump's deeply ingrained, and totally self-centered, world view. It is of no interest to the defeated former president that in the 2000 election – notwithstanding a sudden, bitter and highly questionable loss in the United States Supreme Court – Democratic candidate and former Vice President Al Gore graciously stepped aside and accepted what at that point in time boiled down to something like a 500 vote difference in the popular vote in the single State of Florida. And a questionable difference that was as well, subject as it was to further recounting under State Law!

It is also amusing that – in such a situation – Trump was instinctively borrowing from one of his primary professional mentors, Roy Cohn. Evidently, the lesson he learned from Cohn – aggressive attorney and notoriously unforgiving litigator – was that a "winner" must not shy away from borderline conduct when required to prevail in a legal case or other dispute.

Published on Twitter, @henry_kaufman20, 6/23/23

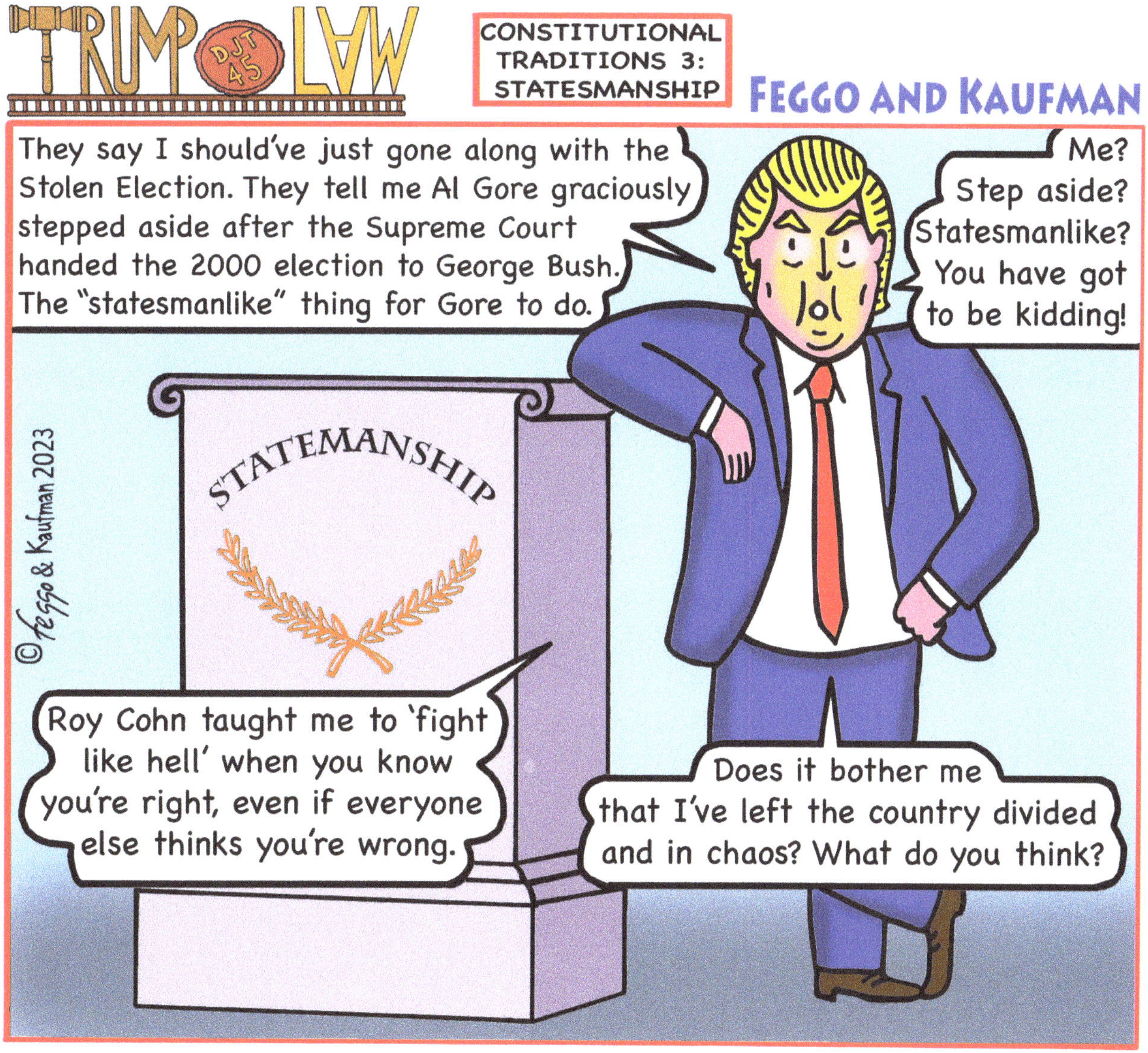

# TRUMP LAW



## FEGGO AND KAUFMAN

Perry & Mason are taking no prisoners here. One might ask: this must be an overstatement! No president could be that crass or venal – right? Perhaps it's just a day to be cynical. Think of it this way: now that we know Trump is not as rich as he has all along been saying, maybe the 100% venality is not all encompassing or at least not totally successful. Donald Trump is asking us to be the judges in 2024.

Just think about what he's shown us in the run-up to that election…

Published on Twitter, @henry_kaufman20, 6/26/23

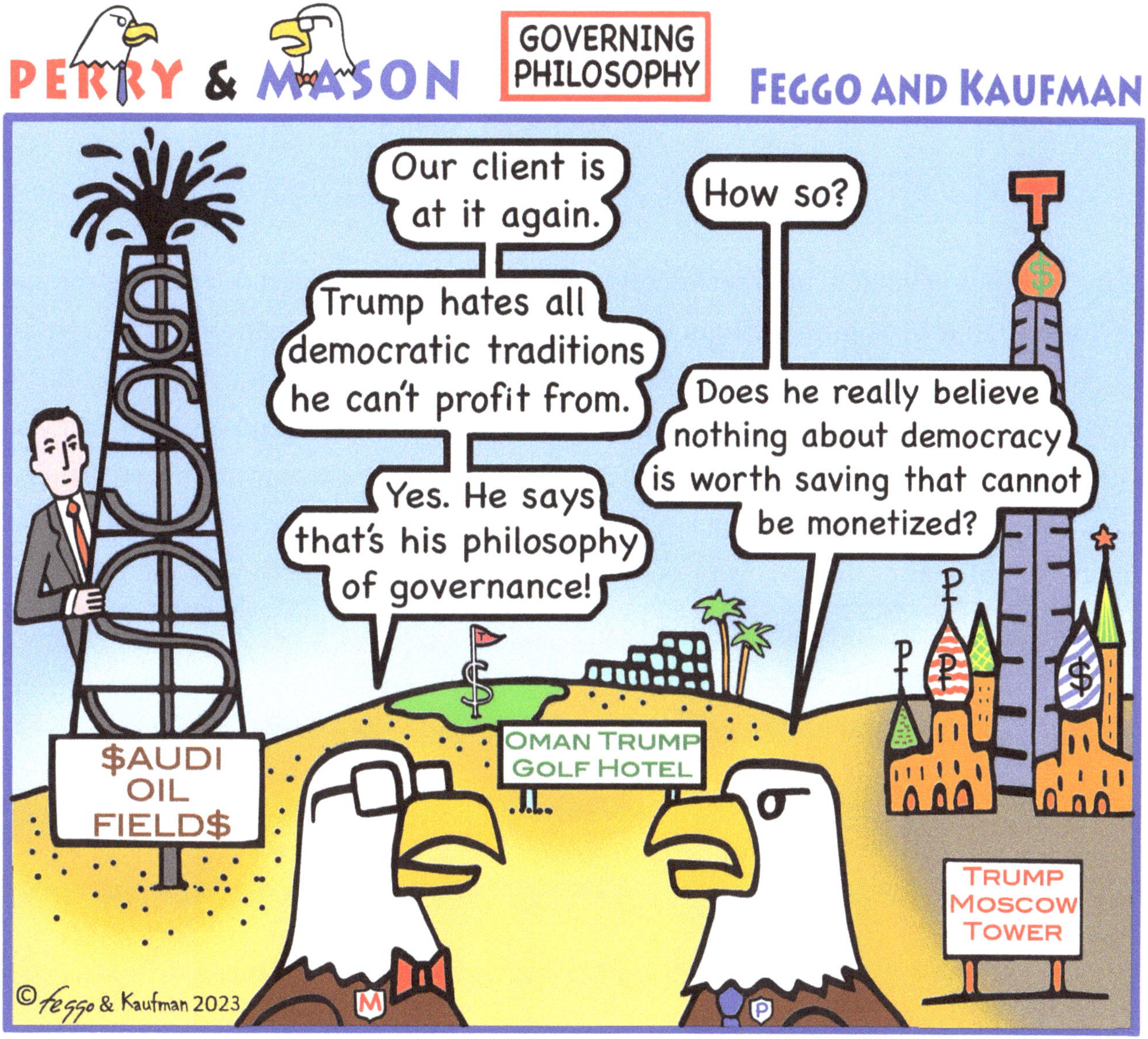

GOVERNING PHILOSOPHY



Our client is at it again.
Trump hates all democratic traditions he can't profit from.
Yes. He says that's his philosophy of governance!
How so?
Does he really believe nothing about democracy is worth saving that cannot be monetized?
$AUDI OIL FIELD$
OMAN TRUMP GOLF HOTEL
TRUMP MOSCOW TOWER
© feggo & Kaufman 2023

Here we find Donald Trump seemingly oblivious to yet another tradition of our great Nation. That is, national unity in time of war. It seems that Trump simply wants to claim credit for international accomplishments that have not even taken place. But note matter what fantasies Trump may envision for the future, right now there is a war going on in the Ukraine, NATO has stepped up to the plate to a great extent to help out, but yet Donald Trump seems to think he knows best. Although no one has ever in the history of war or diplomacy stopped a war in 24 hours – at least without trading for something of exceptional value…

In any event, unfortunately, we can only watch and wait to see how this plays out over time – and including in the 2024 presidential election. God save the United States of America! And, God, please help United States!!

TRUMP LAW
DJT 45
TRADITIONS 4: NATIONAL UNITY IN WARTIME
FEGGO AND KAUFMAN

I call on all Americans to support the war effort in Ukraine. And I'm proud to announce that – after diligent hard work – we have also strengthened the NATO alliance as never before!
The war in Ukraine would be so easy for me to resolve. First, of course Putin wouldn't have dared to start the war if I'd still been President. That's for sure!
And now that Biden has messed everything up, I could still end the war in 24 hours. Mark my words! Does that mean we'd withdraw all US aide to Ukraine and NATO? What do you think? MAGA knows best!
Just leave it to me and my buddy, the Donald, and everything will work out just fine! All power to my revanchist Soviet –I mean Russian, of course– Empire!! What 'collusion'?
© Feggo & Kaufman 2023

As we've noted elsewhere, the concept of democracy and persistent lying by a head of state are wholly at war with one another.

This cartoon is a renewed reminder – based closely on one we previously published from a time during Trump's 2016 presidency – that Donald Trump has no instinct for, nor loyalty to, the truth.

The closest Trump seems to be able to come to something like the "truth" is when he issues a statement that is untrue but that is believed – or least not actively challenged – and that has a continuing, long-term role for Trump that he believes will be helpful to him in advancing some project or another.

In this cartoon, our original "truth meter" ended the 2016 term with 30,573 "false or misleading claims" by Trump during his presidency (as tabulated by the Washington Post Fact Checker). When we published this follow-up cartoon, we had no idea what the exact count had become, but we felt quite safe in updating the meter number into the 40-thousands while still actively spinning.

Published on X, @henry_kaufman20, 7/2/23

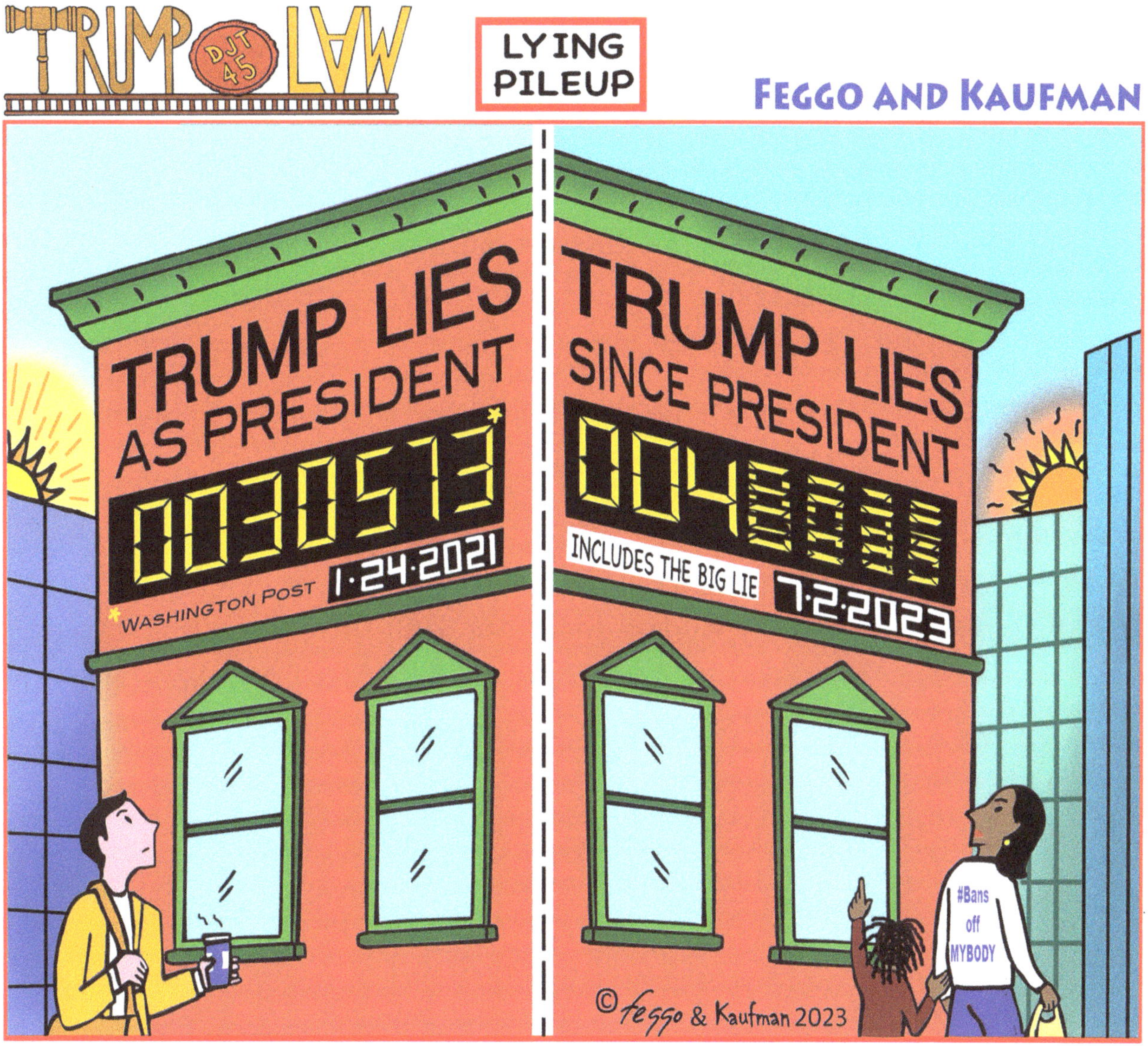

## FEGGO AND KAUFMAN

This sprightly cartoon takes off from a conservative-initiated food fight over the so-called "War on Christmas," which fable Trump made one of the centerpieces of his 2016 campaign. This great war essentially boiled down to a subversive attempt to substitute a seasonal "Happy Holidays" greeting for "Merry Christmas."

More specifically, as illustrated in the cartoon, this was a fight to the finish between "MAGA Patriots" and the "Woke Mob."

N.B.: that Trump made a rare, but fateful marketing error in this cartoon when he held up any old "Holy Bible" instead of putting in a pitch for his new "God Bless the USA" Bible. Only $59.99 (not including shipping and other fees plus one imagines a – 'voluntary' – contribution to Trump's Make America Great Again 2024 Presidential Campaign!

Published on X, @henry_kaufman20, 7/6/23

TRUMP LAW
DJT 45



TRADITIONS 5:
Separation of Church & State



FEGGO AND KAUFMAN



My supporters know I, Donald Trump, single-handedly won the WAR ON CHRISTMAS! Thank god!!
Property of Ivanka
+ BIBLE
ST JOHN'S CHURCH PARISH HOUSE
SUNDAY SERVICES ONLINE
ALL WELCOME!
MERRY CHRISTMAS!
HAPPY HOLIDAYS!
MAGA Patriots
WOKE MOB
©feggo & Kaufman 2023

This beautiful and incisive cartoon well illustrates Donald Trump's blithely self-serving attitude toward the "rule of law."

Trump seems totally unimpressed that one of our great founding fathers, John Adams, has come to illustrate the great democratic rule of law. Indeed, at the very same time Adams is inscribing the rule, Trump is crumpling up another copy of the U.S. Constitution!

Then, Trump embarks on a well-rehearsed and finely-honed rant taking off from his claim of another "witch hunt" and then blaming everything on "Marxists" and "Lunatics."

And finally, the defeated, former president is ready to play his final "trump" card: a very specific threat of riots ("violence on the streets of America"), combined with "potential death and destruction!"

Published on X, @henry_kaufman20, 7/9/23

# TRUMP LAW



## FEGGO AND KAUFMAN

The message of this three-part cartoon is quite clear and simple.

On the day of his inauguration as the 45th President of the United States (1/20/2017), Donald Trump adhered to tradition when he swore the standard oath of office (on the left) – i.e., that he would "preserve, protect and defend the Constitution of the United States."

Yet, at the end of his term of office, Trump purported to single-handedly create a historic level of tumult and uncertainty with his aggressive claim that the 2020 presidential election had been "rigged and stolen!" And at one notable high point of that election denialism, on December 4, 2022, Donald Trump took a historic leap away from U.S. constitutional tradition when he announced (in the second panel of this cartoon, from the highest mountain top) his ultimate position that an allegedly "massive fraud," such as his unproven claim of a rigged and stolen presidential election in 2020, "allows for a termination of rules, regulations and articles – and even of the Constitution!"

And finally, in the right-hand panel, it is this kind of thinking that had led Trump's gang of supporters to assist Trump in his insurrection at the Capitol on January 6, 2021!


Published on X, @henry_kaufman 20, 7/10/23.

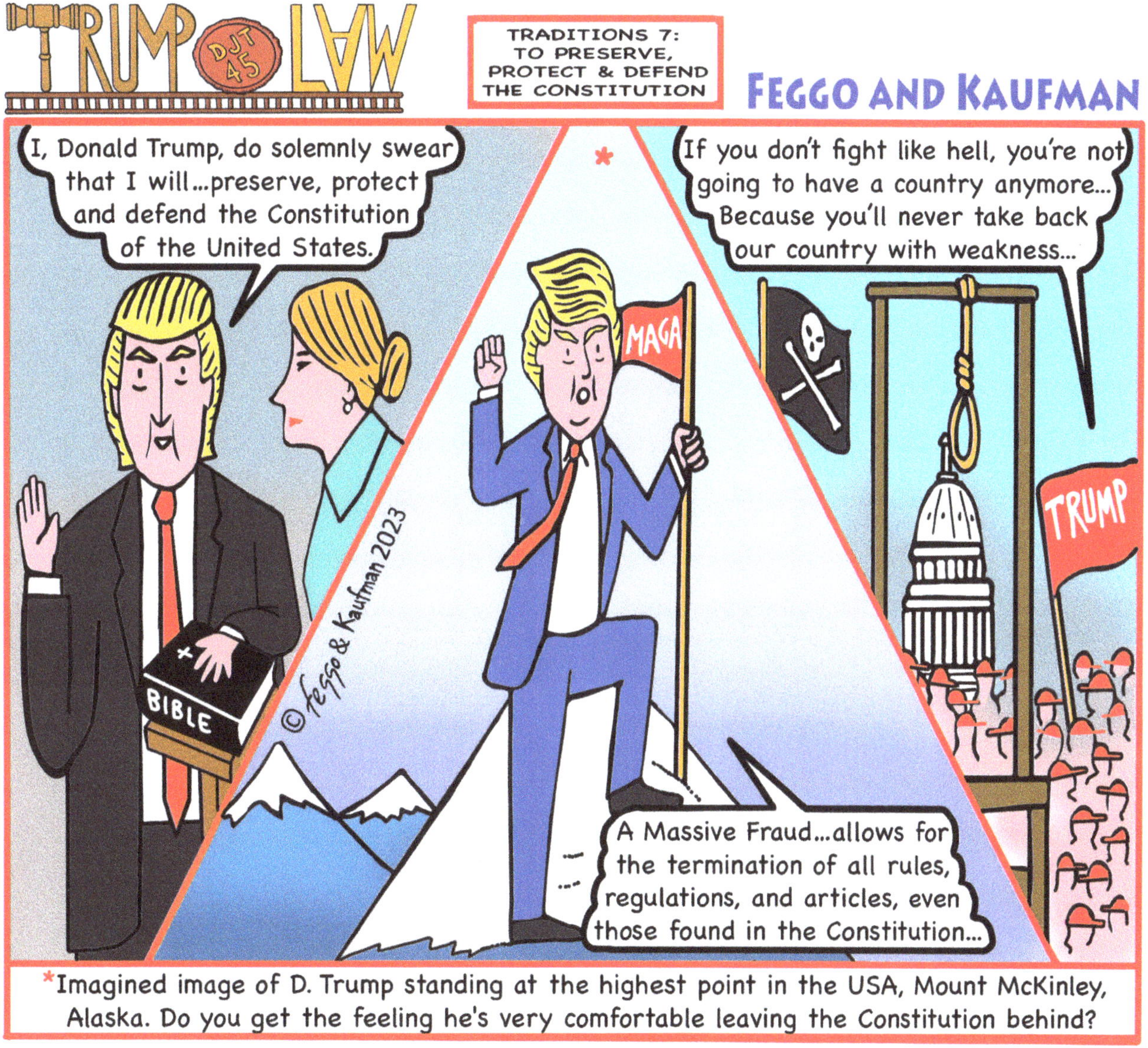

*Imagined image of D. Trump standing at the highest point in the USA, Mount McKinley, Alaska. Do you get the feeling he's very comfortable leaving the Constitution behind?

He's at it again and the Legal Eagles are totally exasperated. Who can possibly blame them? First there was the $5 million verdict for "sexual abuse." Sounds like a lot, for the average Joe. But we are dealing with a billionaire. Allegedly!

Then, as Perry and Mason are lamenting, he did it all over again. Trump was lying about that "Bergdorf Goodman" lady seemingly every time he opened his mouth! With a predictable result – i.e., a separate judgment for defamation!

But this time we were no longer talking about "chump change." How's this one from the second jury? $18.3 million in compensatory damages! Still not shocked? How's $65 million in punitive damages? Total in case a computer is not handy: $83.3 million!!

Yes, I guess Perry & Mason could fairly say they have "an idiot for client!"


Published on  X,@henry_kaufman20, 7/12/23

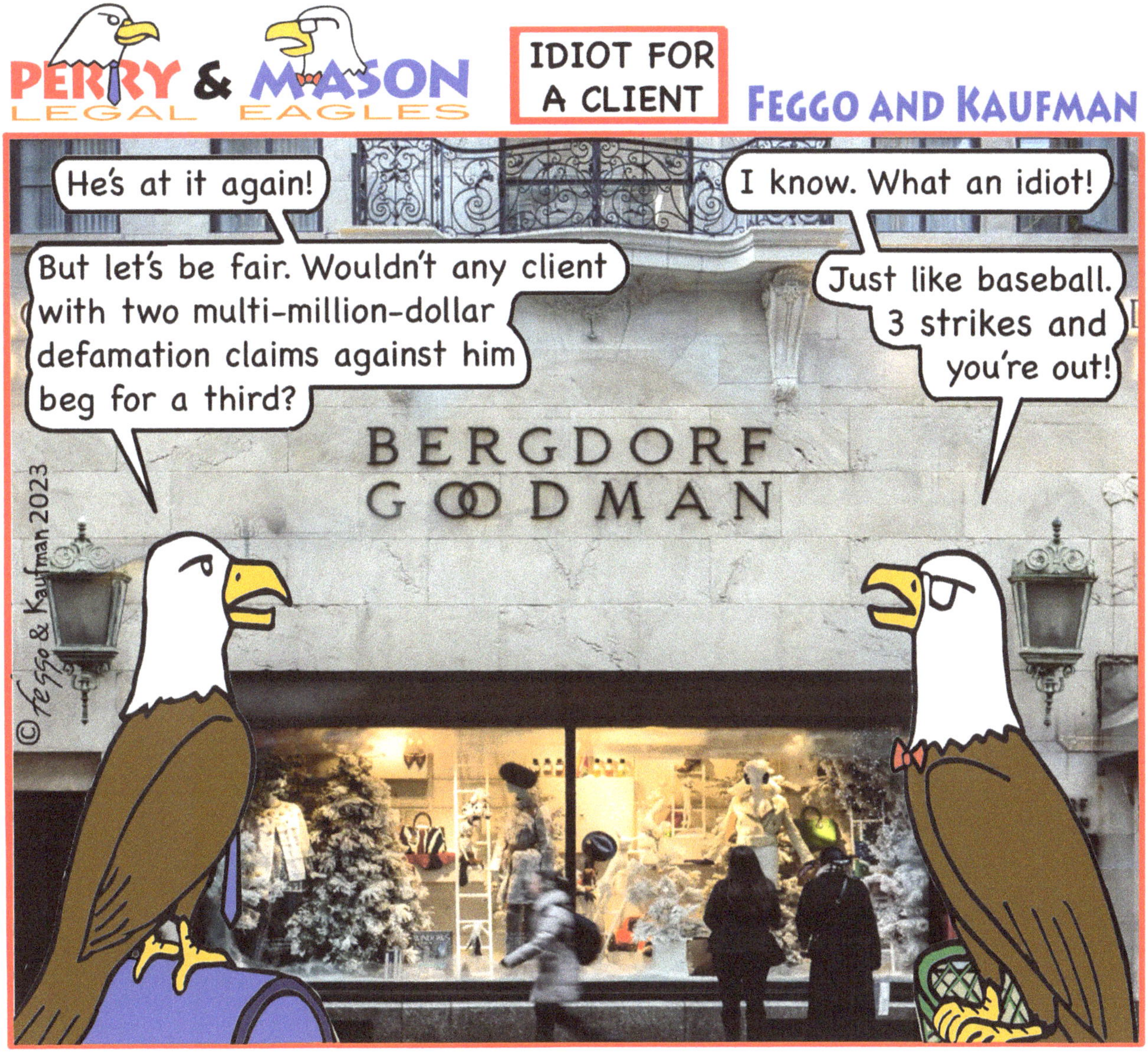

IDIOT FOR A CLIENT

FEGGO AND KAUFMAN

Oh no! Not again!!

Yes, again!!!

Why not spread another baseless, false and defamatory rumor? You're only the former President of the United States!

Perry & Mason have got 45's number …

Published on X, @henry_kaufman20, 7/19/23

PERRY & MASON
LEGAL EAGLES
IDIOT FOR A CLIENT II
FEGGO AND KAUFMAN
Mason, heard the news about our most idiotic client?
What's Trump done this time?
He accused the Special Counsel of drug abuse. Even says Smith "looks like a crackhead."
Because of that cocaine found in the White House recently?
As usual, based on nothing, Trump has accused Hunter and Biden, of "probably" using the cocaine themselves.
When he makes those crazy accusations, who could possibly believe him, much less in his qualifications for a second term as President of the United States?
Good question!
©Feggo & Kaufman 2023
P
M

A documentary flashback to the day Donald Trump had to leave the White House. Why? His term of office was over!

As we envision it, the drama is operatic – or at least Shakespearean!!

As Legal Eagle, Perry, puts it so aptly:  "a President who attempts to remain in office after his Term is over violates his sacred oath." His oath is to "preserve, protect and defend" the Constitution which, of course, includes term limits for our Presidents.

Published on X, @henry_kaufman20, 7/23/23

# PERRY & MASON LEGAL EAGLES — OATH OF OFFICE — FEGGO AND KAUFMAN

Another rudimentary lesson in the law of the United States Presidency. Didn't Donald Trump have advisors who could explain this to him?

You may ask: how could it be this simple when we've had months and years of chaotic division over who was elected President of the United States on November 3, 2020?

Look it up!

Published on X, @henry_kaufman20, 7/26/23

PERRY & MASON
LEGAL EAGLES
ONLY WAY TO BE ELECTED
FEGGO AND KAUFMAN



The U.S. President wins an election by receiving a majority of the states' Electoral College votes.
And each state has an established agency that runs its own elections.
How does a President overrule the official Electoral College result?
UNITED STATES OF TRUMP INC.
He doesn't! Unless we'd like to tear up the Constitution and become a wholly-owned subsidiary of the Trump Organization!
© Feggo & Kaufman 2023

Cartoonists never like to be stuck in a rut. So as we began detecting a "countdown" feeling in the air regarding the 2024 election – still more than a year in advance – we felt the need to put our own spin on the presidential countdown.

First of all, it's kind of mind-blowing to see here that we started the Countdown Calendar project when there were still 460 days(!) to go before the 2024 presidential election. My how fast time is passing!!

If you have an eye for these kinds of things you may also get a sense that we were in a bit of a struggle to try to conceive of and organize various elements of the Election Cartoon Calendar. Of course, we knew we wanted to have an election theme. Thus, the traditional, "in-person," curtained election booth. We also knew we wanted to have a countdown element. And beyond that we were not quite certain.

As you will see, the initial resolution was to have Donald Trump portrayed as one of the contestants – he had already made his record-setting (for early-ness) announcement – and for some reason, on this particular date, we still had in mind some of the most prominent election interference leaders. Here, Rudy Giuliani and the "Kraken" lady, Sidney Powell. (It was only later that Powell was indicted – and then took an early plea – in the Georgia election interference case.)


Published on X, @henry_kaufman20, 8/2/23

# 460 Days to Election Day

&

Here is Donald Trump in Court, torn between two strong instincts in his trial conduct and comportment.

First, compliance for self-preservation. I know this doesn't sound like the Donald we know. But have no fear, even in the context of this representation of Trump's split personality, the "real" Donald is not hard to detect and not long hidden!

And, as we all know from long experience, Donald Trump's true personality is bound to win out – whether silently or out loud. And the silent stuff will not remain silent for very long!

Published on X, @henry_kaufman20, 8/10/23

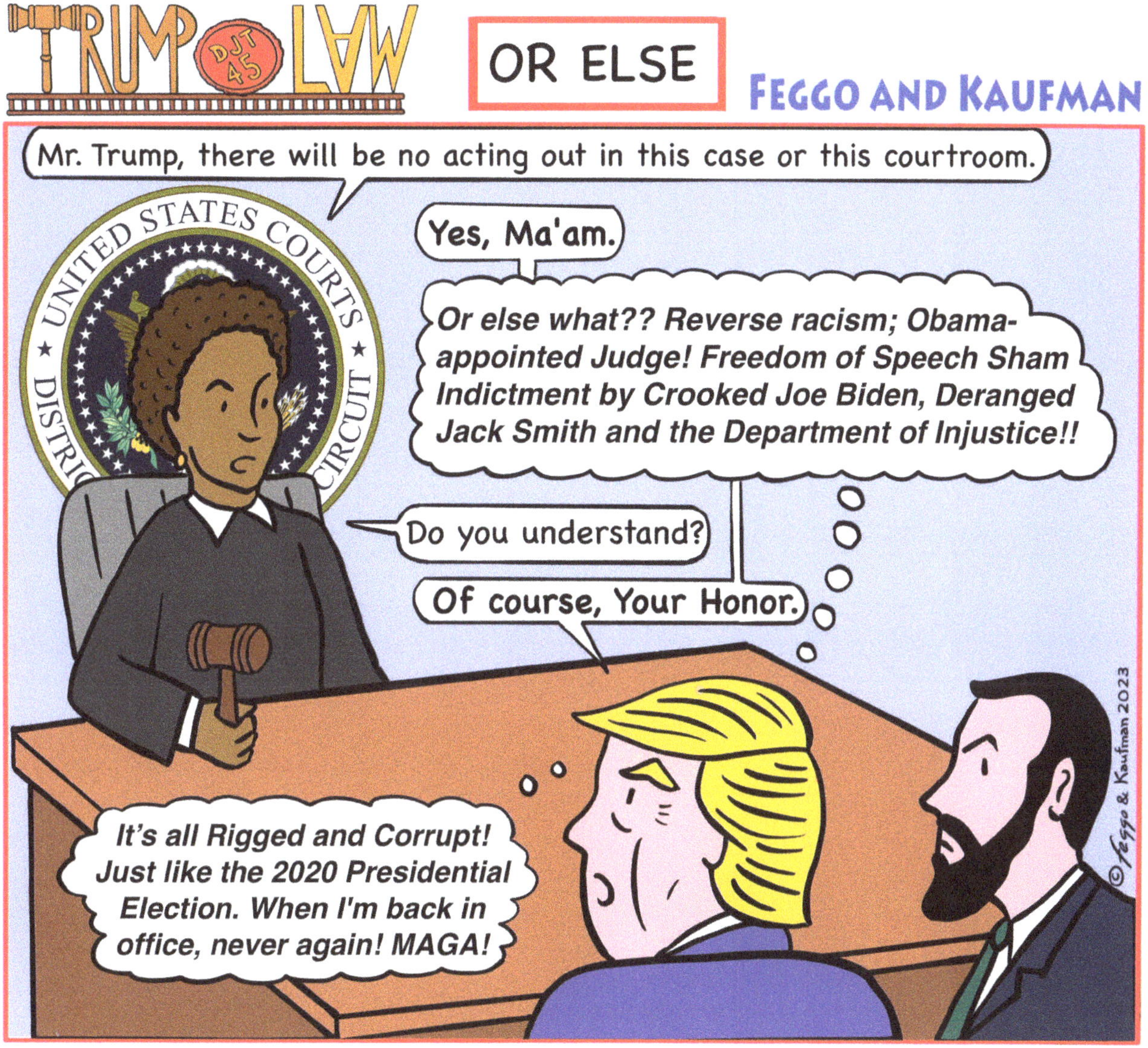

# OR ELSE

**FEGGO AND KAUFMAN**

After many, many months of Trump-initiated delays, in most of his cases, some of the humor has gone out of this particular cartoon.

Nonetheless, with only one major criminal case having broken free from the persistent, repeated deadlock and delays (the New York State "hush-money" trial), there will doubtless be more than one grain of truth in this cartoon, still to come.

And, in any event, when focusing on some of the outlandish time extensions sought on his behalf by Donald Trump's attorneys, it is kind of fun to think about a Trump trip to Mars as a possible excuse for more delay!

Published on X, @henry_kaufman20, 9/1/23

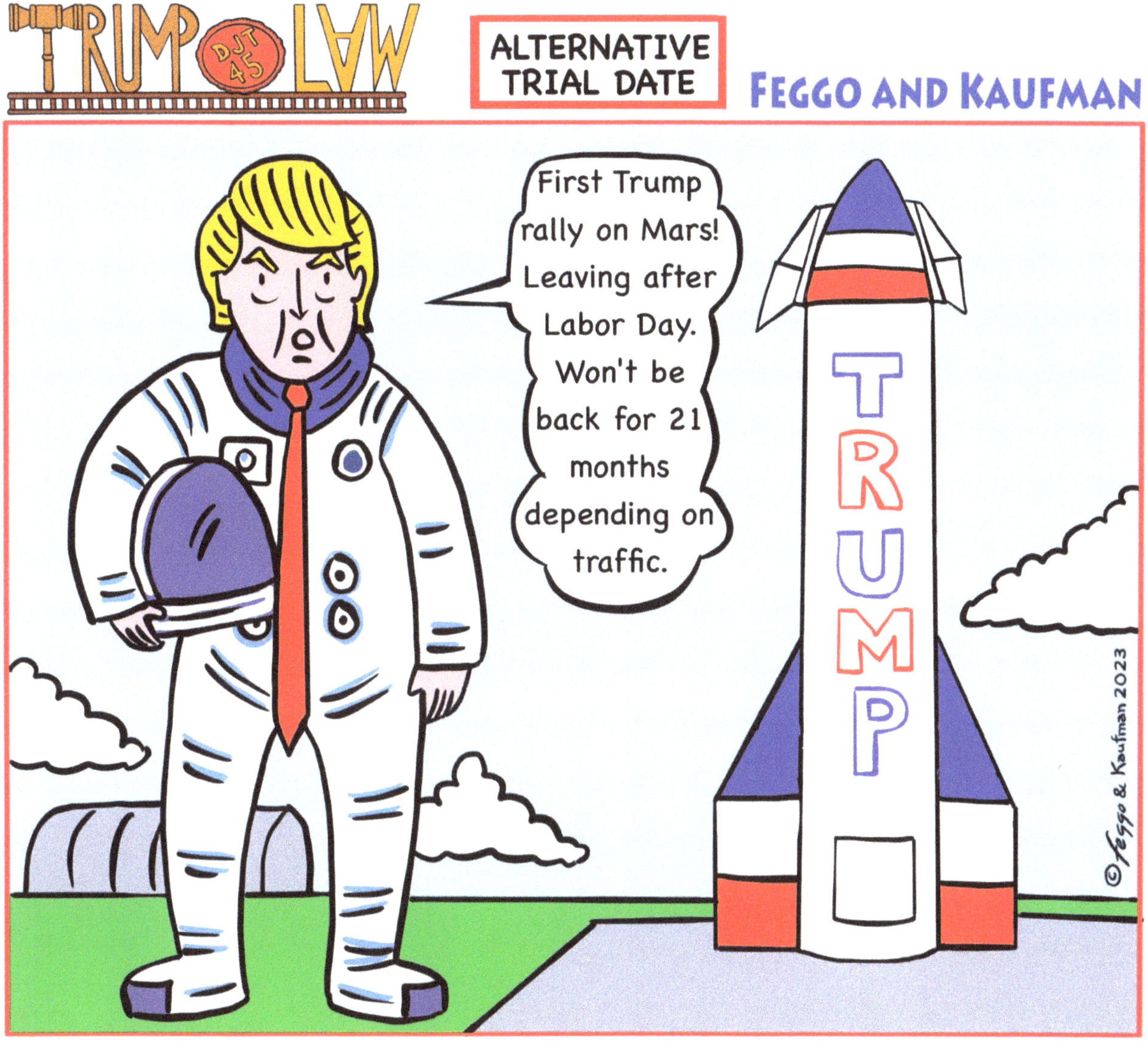

## FEGGO AND KAUFMAN

Trump and Putin "in bed together." Sounds about right to these authors. And the two do seem quite comfortable there, in our cartoon fantasy, having similarly been portrayed in the same bed in one of our earliest TrumpTruth cartoons. That is the one where Putin opines to his comrade Donald: "only weak leaders actually count ballots!" Suggestion taken!!

Published on X, @henry_kaufman20, 8/23/23

TRUMP LAW
DJT 45
IN BED TOGETHER
FEGGO AND KAUFMAN
You've always been the apple of my eye, товарищ!*
I know, comrade. But isn't it amazing how so few in my MAGA base understand that – or care!
©feggo & Kaufman 2023
* "comrade" in Russian

Donnie and Vladimir in bed together – again!

But this time it's Donnie who's taking the lead. Thinking about the bail money he actually had to put up in one of his cases. Imagine that! A former president of the United States!! And the hard prison time that may ultimately be awaiting him!!!

Oh, how much Donnie would prefer simply to stay in Russia, in bed with his good friend Vladimir! Vladimir – one of the richest men in the world. Vladimir – whose bedroom happens to have a very nice view of the gold domed Cathedrals of Moscow. Vladimir – who is trying to entice his Donnie back into bed!! A place one would never have imagined for a "conservative" leader of the American Republican Party!!!

Published on X, @henry_kaufman20, 8/25/23

# TRUMP LAW



FLIGHT RISK

## FEGGO AND KAUFMAN

An open and shut case – at least in the real world. But not Donald Trump's world! Chaos and controversy are apparently indispensable parts of his toolkit!!

Published on X, @henry_kaufman20 , 9/9/23; and @DavidCayJ, 9/18/23

TRUMP LAW
DJT 45
DECISION 2024
FEGGO AND KAUFMAN
Congratulations. Looks like you're our candidate -again!
MAGA AGAIN
REPUBLICAN NATIONAL COMMITTEE
Only one requirement this time. But it's a tough one. If you run, you must promise to accept the result of the election!
Are you kidding? That's only in a democracy!
©Feggo & Kaufman 2023

The defeated former President is still lying about the outcome of the 2020 election to the chagrin of his Legal Eagles who, it is evident, are aware that no other defeated president in American history has attempted to cling to power – based much less on a glaring lie! And, in the meantime, Perry & Mason are both perched on an extension of Donald Trump's nose, just like Pinocchio!

Published on X, @henry_kaufman20, 9/1/23

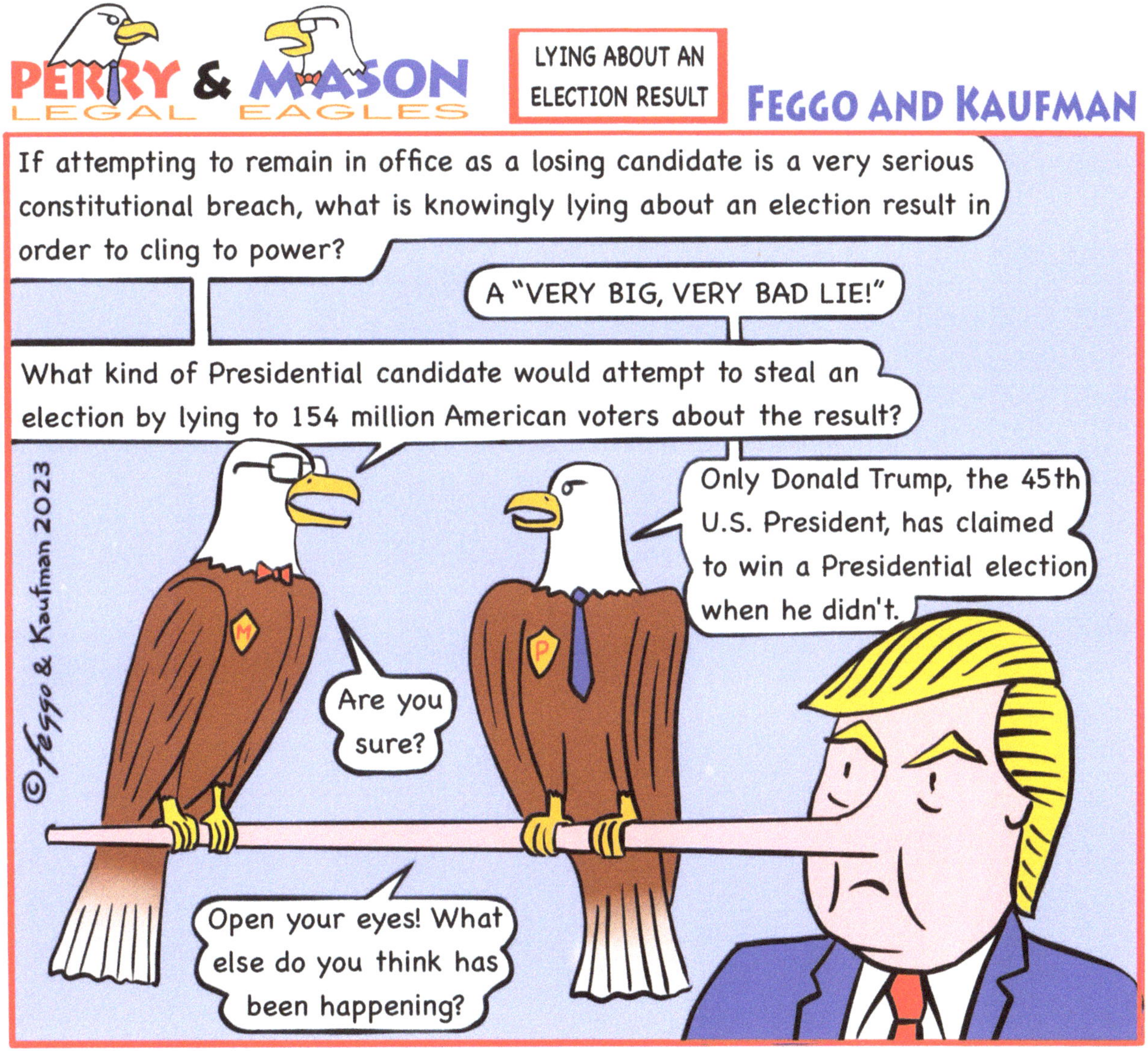

FEGGO AND KAUFMAN

This cartoon presents a more general commentary on how Trump would run a business if he applied the same techniques as when he was President. Very simple: Doctor to patient on entering the dental office, "this will be painless!"
On exiting the office, *PAIN*!

Published on X, @henry_kaufman20, 9/12/23

TRUMP LAW
DJT 45



BAIT & SWITCH
FEGGO AND KAUFMAN
PAINLESS DENTAL SURGERY
ENTRANCE
EXIT
Great business model!
How I've always operated!
© feggo & Kaufman 2023

Perry & Mason appear to know by heart, and point by point, all of their client's excesses when commenting on his legal opponents – whether he is gagged or ungagged. The Legal Eagles are creatively proposing that they – rather than he – read from the Trump "script" in order to protect their client from the further legal consequences of his intemperate comments and his lack of control.

Published on X, @henry_kaufman20, 9/23/23

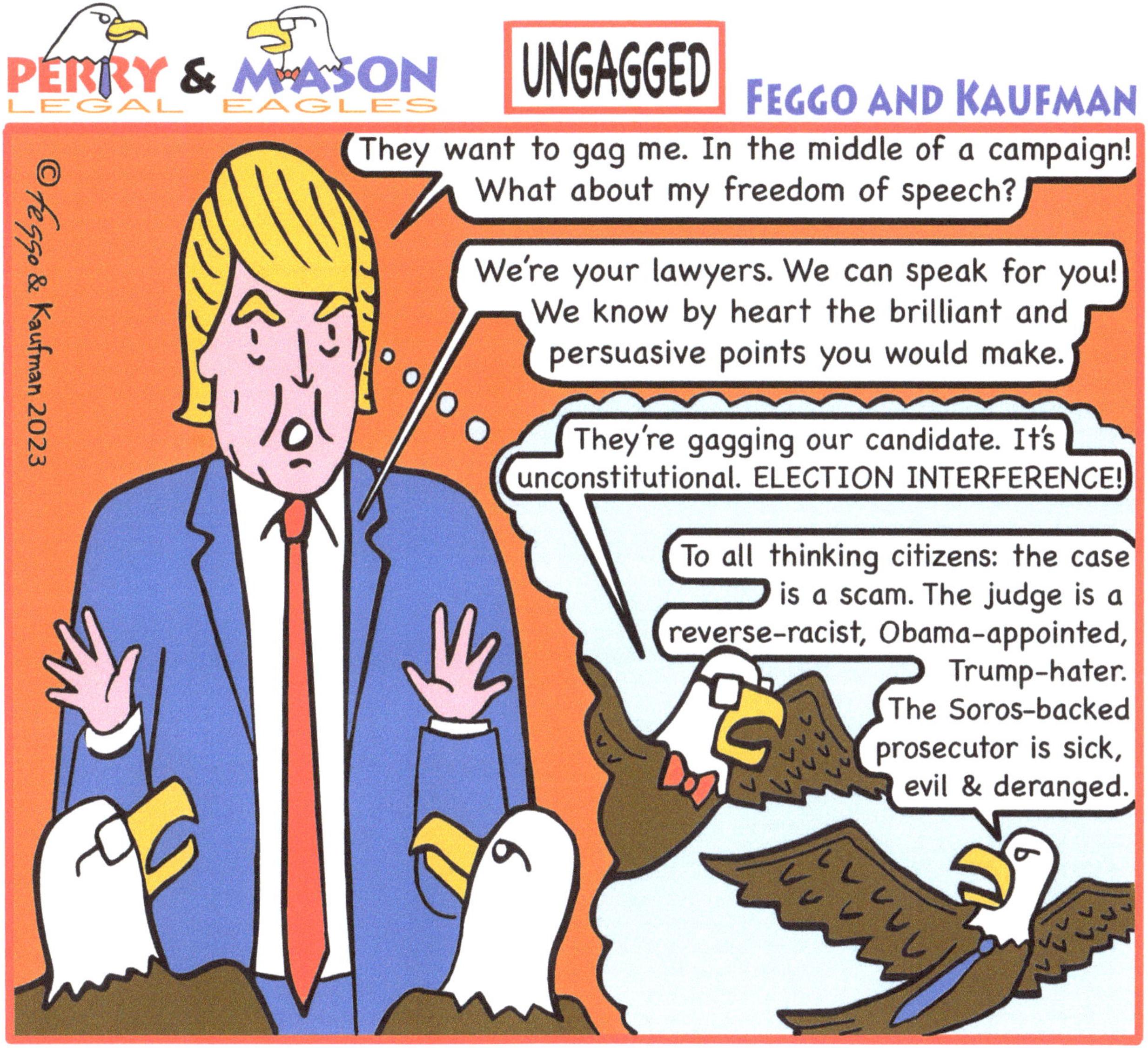

# PERRY & MASON — FEGGO AND KAUFMAN

Clearly, the tables have been turning against Donald Trump, his real estate "empire" and his other businesses! But exactly how all of this will play out, in the context of his widespread "assets," still very much remains to be seen.

In all likelihood, we now know, any Trump financial catastrophe will not be as simple as liquidating a single building or golf club. For example, one "expert" on Trump's finances recently stated, with great certainty, that Trump actually owns very little of his best-known, landmark building, Trump Tower (depicted here). Indeed, his current stake may be limited the famous escalator, a few first-floor leases, and his own equally-famously overestimated 30,000 square foot condominium home – or is it 10,000 square feet?

A statement in response from the defeated former president: "When you're as rich and successful as I, Donald Trump, it's really hard to recall so many room dimensions! So don't put me parading on Fifth Avenue in a sandwich board quite yet! MAGA!"

Published on X, @henry_kaufman20, 9/30/23

TRUMP LAW
DJT 45
TABLES TURNED
FEGGO AND KAUFMAN
TRUMP TOWER
Fifth Ave
LOST OUR LEASE!
50% OFF SALE!
© feggo & Kaufman 2023

Keep in mind: As the nation is reminded almost every day, when Donald Trump says something you can count on it! And when Donald Trump guarantees something you can count on it! And especially when Donald Trump backs up what he's saying with statistics, facts and figures, you can take it to the bank!

So, when it comes to Donald Trump's claim that he alone defeated ISIS, during his term of office, you need have no doubt! No doubt of what? No doubt that it will not be true or at least entirely true.

Never forget the 30,000 lies …

Published on X, @henry_kaufman20, 10/17/23

TRUMP LAW
DJT 45



Trump v. ISIS
(I ALONE!)



FEGGO AND KAUFMAN

Forget that map. Trust me, Obama Hussein did nothing vs. ISIS. 0%!



I ordered my generals to get the job done I told them to slaughter ISIS like dogs, 100%! Then we got the hell out of there.



© Feggo & Kaufman 2023



TRUMP
US ARMY



CHRONICLING THE DEFEAT OF ISLAMIC STATE UNDER OBAMA, TRUMP AND PUTIN
2014-2016 ISIS Rollback Under Obama
2017-2019 ISIS Rollback Under Trump
2015-2019 ISIS Rollback Under Putin/Assad
TURKEY
Jarabulus   Kobane   Tal Abyad
Azaz   Manbij   Al Hasakah
Afrin   Al Bab   Tishrin Dam   Sinjar   Mosul
Aleppo   Raqqa   Al Badi   Tal Afar   Erbil
Idlib   Makhmur
Latakia   Al Tabqah Dam   Al Qayyarah   Kirkuk
SYRIA   Deir   Remaining ISIS Forces   Sulaymaniyah
Tartus   IRAQ   Hawija
Al Mayadin   Baiji   Tikrit
Palmyra   Hajin   Rawa
Abu Kamal   Samarra
Qaim   Haditha
Remaining ISIS Forces   Hit   Baqubah
Al Tanf   Ramadi
Baghdad
Fallujah
55-km Deconfliction Zone   Jurf Al Sakhar
MEDITERRANEAN SEA
ISIS CALIPHATE



So we totally eliminated ISIS. And that's why the Oct. 7 attack by Hamas would not have happened -zero chance- if the 2020 election was not rigged & stolen.

By now, we all know that Donald Trump is no fan of the truth unless it serves his purposes. Imagine what he thinks of statistics!

In this cartoon Trump is confronted with data undermining, point by point, the overstatements he has made, as President, and as Commander-In-Chief, about his supposed, long-standing and oft-repeated claim that it was he – and he alone – who vanquished ISIS during his term in office. And that Obama had done nothing about ISIS, "0%!"

Low and behold those pesky statistics tell a completely different story! See the data for yourself: in maps and in multiple news stories, Donald Trump's lies are just what we are saying they are: LIES!

Published on X, @henry_kaufman20, 10/20/23

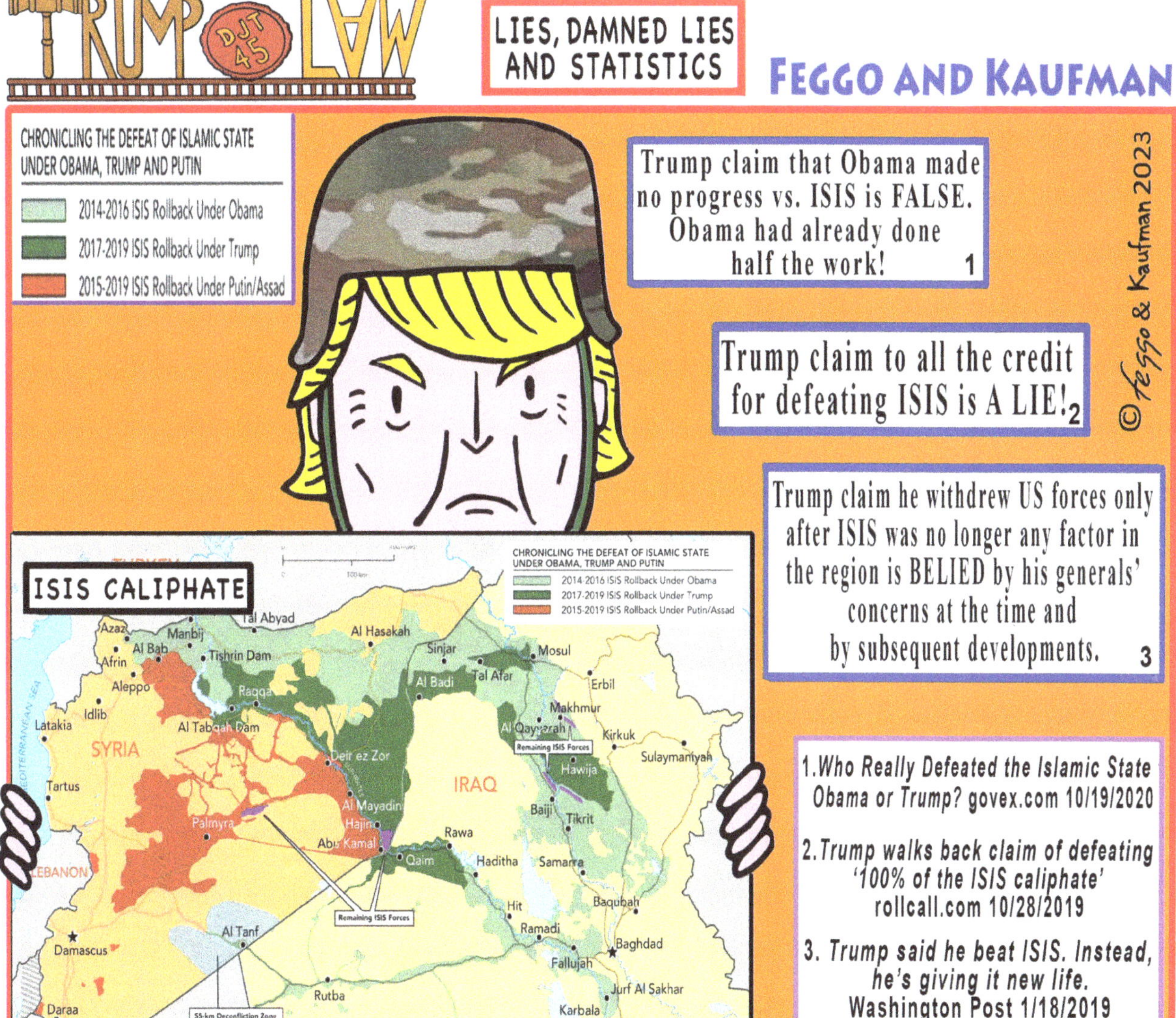

TRUMP LAW
DJT 45
LIES, DAMNED LIES AND STATISTICS
FEGGO AND KAUFMAN
CHRONICLING THE DEFEAT OF ISLAMIC STATE UNDER OBAMA, TRUMP AND PUTIN
2014-2016 ISIS Rollback Under Obama
2017-2019 ISIS Rollback Under Trump
2015-2019 ISIS Rollback Under Putin/Assad
© Feggo & Kaufman 2023
Trump claim that Obama made no progress vs. ISIS is FALSE. Obama had already done half the work! 1
Trump claim to all the credit for defeating ISIS is A LIE! 2
Trump claim he withdrew US forces only after ISIS was no longer any factor in the region is BELIED by his generals' concerns at the time and by subsequent developments. 3
ISIS CALIPHATE
CHRONICLING THE DEFEAT OF ISLAMIC STATE UNDER OBAMA, TRUMP AND PUTIN
2014-2016 ISIS Rollback Under Obama
2017-2019 ISIS Rollback Under Trump
2015-2019 ISIS Rollback Under Putin/Assad
TURKEY
Azaz
Manbij
Tal Abyad
Al Hasakah
Sinjar
Mosul
Afrin
Al Bab
Tishrin Dam
Al Badi
Tal Afar
Erbil
Aleppo
Raqqa
Makhmur
Al Tabqah Dam
Al Qayyarah
Kirkuk
Idlib
Latakia
Deir ez Zor
Remaining ISIS Forces
Hawija
Sulaymaniyah
SYRIA
IRAQ
Tartus
Al Mayadin
Baiji
Tikrit
Palmyra
Hajin
Rawa
Abu Kamal
Qaim
Haditha
Samarra
Remaining ISIS Forces
Hit
Baqubah
Al Tanf
Ramadi
LEBANON
Damascus
Baghdad
Fallujah
Daraa
Rutba
Jurf Al Sakhar
55-km Deconfliction Zone
Karbala
MEDITERRANEAN SEA
100 km
1. Who Really Defeated the Islamic State Obama or Trump? govex.com 10/19/2020
2. Trump walks back claim of defeating '100% of the ISIS caliphate' rollcall.com 10/28/2019
3. Trump said he beat ISIS. Instead, he's giving it new life. Washington Post 1/18/2019

Donald Trump is clashing with the Legal Eagles again, as always. And, as always, he's got a lot on his mind; with much of it evidently never shared with his attorneys. In the New York civil fraud case, Trump is already convinced that his former attorney and "fixer," Michael Cohen, has "choked like a dog" on the witness stand and can now be deemed totally incredible. Still, turning to another of his multiple cases, he worries about his former Chief of Staff, Mark Meadows, as a possible witness against him in the stolen election cases. In the meantime, his judge is a "Trump-hater," according to Donald.

What's a spectacularly successful ex-President to do??


Published on X, @henry_kaufman20, 10/27/23

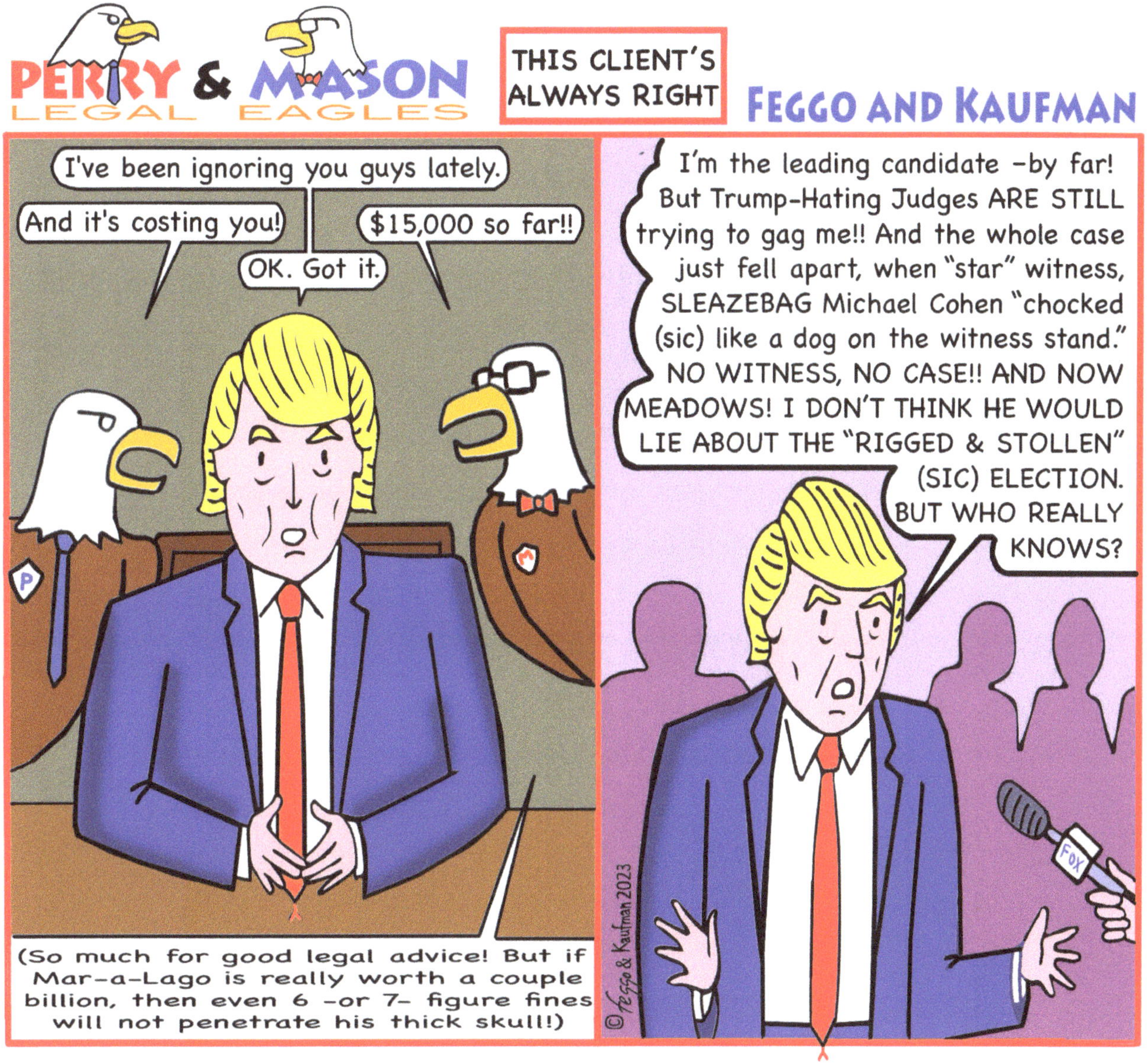

# PERRY & MASON — LEGAL EAGLES

## THIS CLIENT'S ALWAYS RIGHT

## FEGGO AND KAUFMAN

Have got to admit, it's quite amusing to contemplate Donald Trump's answering machine! Here, we imagine both the opening message (about him really winning the 2020 election "in a landslide", of course he!) and the extension choices available to the caller.

On this machine, the general category is "witchhunts." No surprise there! Then, a series of follow-up message options reflect some of Trump's favorite, never-ending concerns: Trump-hating judges;  and prosecutors, deranged or racist. Then he turns to his c oncerns about RINO's, or Democrats, including of course socialists, communists or fascists; and then finally he attempts to accommodate any concern about possible violation of "gag orders."

Once again, what else is a defeated former President to do? And you really cannot get good help these days, for sure!


Published on X, @henry_kaufman20, 11/10/23

TRUMP LAW
DJT 45
TRUMP'S ANSWERING MACHINE
FEGGO AND KAUFMAN
© Feggo & Kaufman 2023
This is your favorite rigged & stolen, but really-relected-in-a-landslide, President. I'm not here now. Leave a message. MAGA!
If your call's about 'witchhunts,' your choices have not changed:
-For rants about Trump-hating judges, press '1'.
-About deranged or racist prosecutors, press '2'.
-About turncoat 'RINO's', press '3'.
-About any Democrat, socialist, communist or fascist, press '4',
or -If any Court has just imposed, or has reinstated, a gag order against me, hang up and log onto TruthSocial/Old Trump Posts!

This cartoon, created shortly after the initial event, identified – as many others had – Trump trying out his fascist waterwings in order – evidently – to soften up his base and the American people – for a turn toward his right wing, authoritarian approach to governing.

In this regard, Trump did not start small. His use of the term "vermin" rocketed him right to the top of the authoritarian playbook! Because that word echoed language often used by Adolf Hitler in his march toward the Nazification of Germany and the dehumanization of those who ultimately became victims of the Nazi genocide.

And in case anybody was sleeping – or did not believe what they or others had heard – Trump's "vermin" reference was soon followed by another Hitlerian trope. This one being Donald Trump's claim that "immigration… is a very sad thing for our country"! Because… – and then the genocidal punchline – "[immigration] is poisoning the blood of our country."

This, in a heretofore democratic nation, which took pride in its ability to attract and to assimilate refugees with a love for democracy and the United States of America!

Published on X, @henry_kaufman20, 11/14/23

TRUMP LAW
DJT 45
VERMIN
FEGGO AND KAUFMAN
TRUMP ANIMAL WORLD
PESKY LITTLE CRITTERS
RATS, MICE, COCKROACHES, SLUGS, CENTIPEDES, WORMS, PARASITES, LICE, BUGS, FLEAS, TICKS, SPIDERS
Call these 'VERMIN.' There will be lines around the block! And prepare cages for communists, Marxists, fascists and radical left thugs.
But Mr. President, 'vermin' is also a terrible ethnic slur associated with Nazi genocide!
Who hired this guy? Is this Disney World? Or TRUMP World??
© Feggo & Kaufman 2023

Actually, we confess, by all indications this cartoon has been built on a completely false factual premise. Apparently, Trump does not himself do his own emails or posting online.

But – however the material is actually reported through some scribe or another – the essential point is that Trump is an online dervish of negativity and outrage. I guess we may need a new expression for "carpal tunnel syndrome!" One conveying what Trump apparently does every hour of every day – but without suggesting there is an immediate phone or other devise at hand for Trump to do that posting.

And what is true about this cartoon – for sure! – is that Trump "can't keep up" with all of the trash that emanates from his mouth and his mind!

Published on X, @henry_kaufman20, 12/4/23

# TRUMP CAN'T KEEP UP

## FEGGO AND KAUFMAN

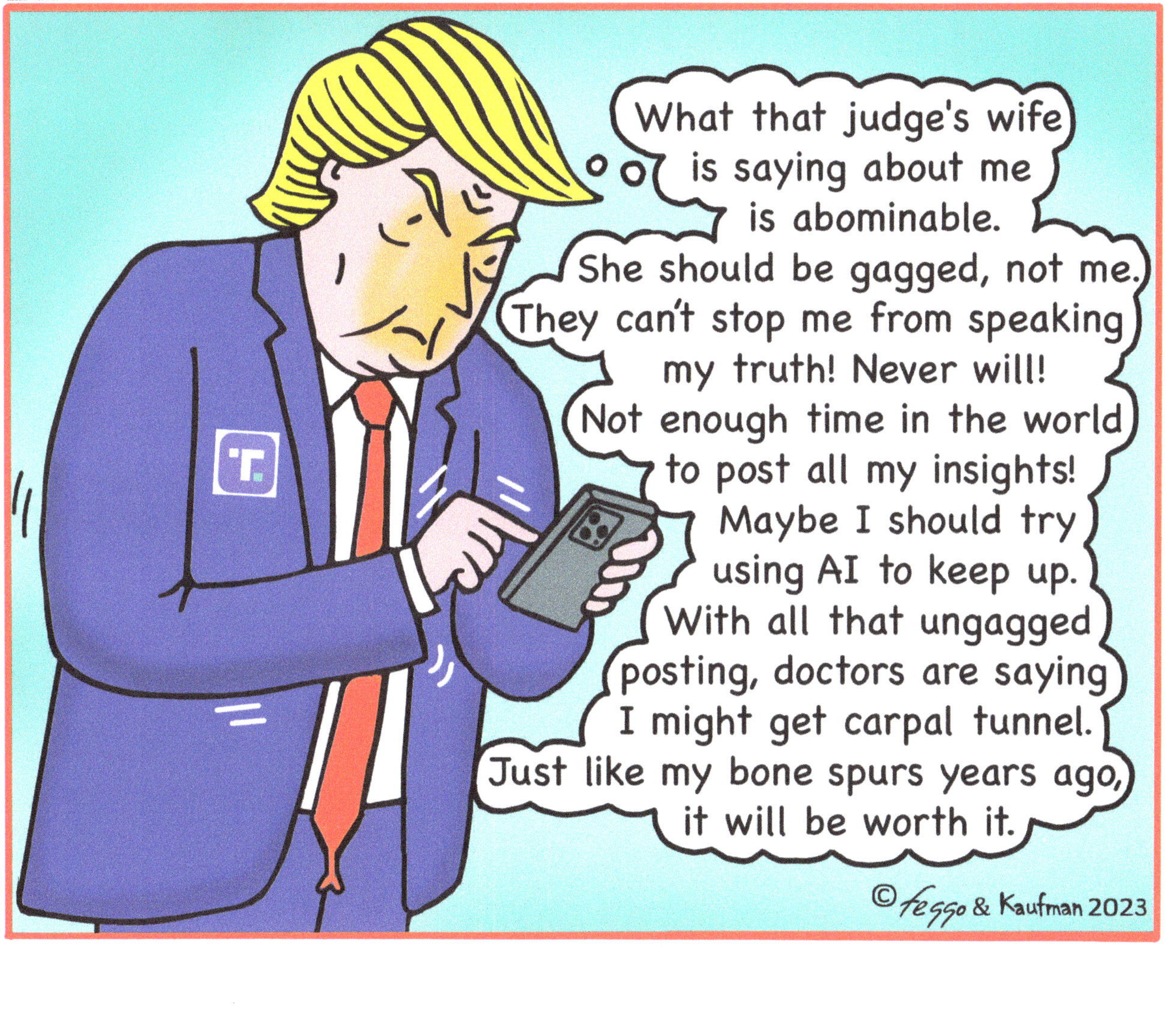

This cartoon strives to make a supremely important point. Donald Trump likes to argue that the criminal and other charges against him – in particular those arising out of January 6 – should be considered "election interference." What brilliant mental gymnastics!

Because it was Donald Trump who actually spent most of his Presidential time and energy – both before and after the 2020 election – attempting to interfere with the election of Joe Biden!

This point is too important to not be repeated: "It was Donald Trump who actually spent most of his presidential time and energy – both before and after the 2020 election – doing everything in his power to wrongfully interfere with the election of Joe Biden, based on what were actually indisputable findings – made by the designated local and state agencies assigned and committed to do just that – as to the real results of the 2020 presidential election!

To be understood, perhaps this needs an analogy. How about: crazy man throws himself in front of a speeding subway train. Miraculously, he survives, although many other people on the train are injured. Who is responsible for the "subway interference?" The crazy man who originally caused the accident? Or the police and law enforcement who later brought charges to punish the crazy guy and to prevent his "subway interference" from happening again?

And finally, please read this cartoon carefully. It highlights several of the ways that it was Donald Trump – and not the Democratic opposition – who started the election interference and who has continued it to this very day!

Published on X, @henry_kaufman20, 12/18/23

TRUMP LAW
DJT 45
THE ACTUAL ELECTION INTERFERENCE
FEGGO AND KAUFMAN
"There will only be a peaceful transition of power if the election is not rigged or stolen." (Fox News Sunday, 7/19/20)
"This is a major fraud on our Nation. We were getting ready to win this election. Frankly we did win this election." (Post-election eve remarks, 11/5/20, 2:20 AM)
"We won in a landslide. We will never give up, we will never concede. You don't concede when there's theft involved. And if you don't fight like hell, you're not going to have a country anymore." (Trump, The White House Ellipse, 1/6/21)
"All I want to find is 11,780 votes ..." (Trump recorded telephone conversation w/ Ga. Secretary of State, 1/2/21)
© Feggo & Kaufman 2023

It turns out there has been a law on the books – and not just any old law books, but recorded in an Amendment to the United States Constitution (Amend. XIV, Sec. III) – providing a remedy that disqualifies any any "insurrectionist" who has previously taken an oath of office to protect and defend the Constitution from holding office again! And, yes, that constitutional amendment is 155 years old. And it was adopted in response to the Civil War and its aftermath.

It must have come as a shock to the Trump insurrectionists to realize that their actions could well have disqualified Donald Trump from ever running for federal office again! The shock was even greater to the extent that one state could in theory have potentially disqualified Donald Trump from running not only in its state's primary, but potentially nationwide.

In this case Donald Trump's vigorous complaints sailed up to the United States Supreme Court where the Court unanimously (with a couple of clarifying concurrences) refused to recognize the possibility that one state could disqualify a national candidate in – of all things – a national Presidential election! Whether there will be any meaningful implications left, flowing from 14 – 3, remains to be seen.

Published on X, @henry_kaufman20, 12/20/23

TRUMP LAW
DJT 45
MORE "ELECTION INTERFERENCE"
FEGGO AND KAUFMAN



Amendment 14, Section 3
No person ...
shall hold any office ...
under the United States ...
who, having previously
taken an oath
to support the Constitution ...
shall have engaged
in insurrection ...
against the same ...
July 9, 1868
© Feggo & Kaufman 2023
Those devious Dems!
They've been waiting
to spring this one
on Trump for more
than 155 years!
ELECTION RIGGING!!

The Nation has been learning how Donald Trump often manages to turn a seemingly sincere "holiday greetings" into a vociferous attack on those he views as his "enemies."

Here is just one actual example, out of many. In which we suggest probable reasons for Trump's hair-triggered anger: will he be going to jail instead of the White House? Only a saint could resist vociferously complaining about that frightening possibility.

And, for sure, Donald Trump is no saint!


Published on X, @henry_kaufman20, 12/29/23

TRUMP LAW
DJT 45

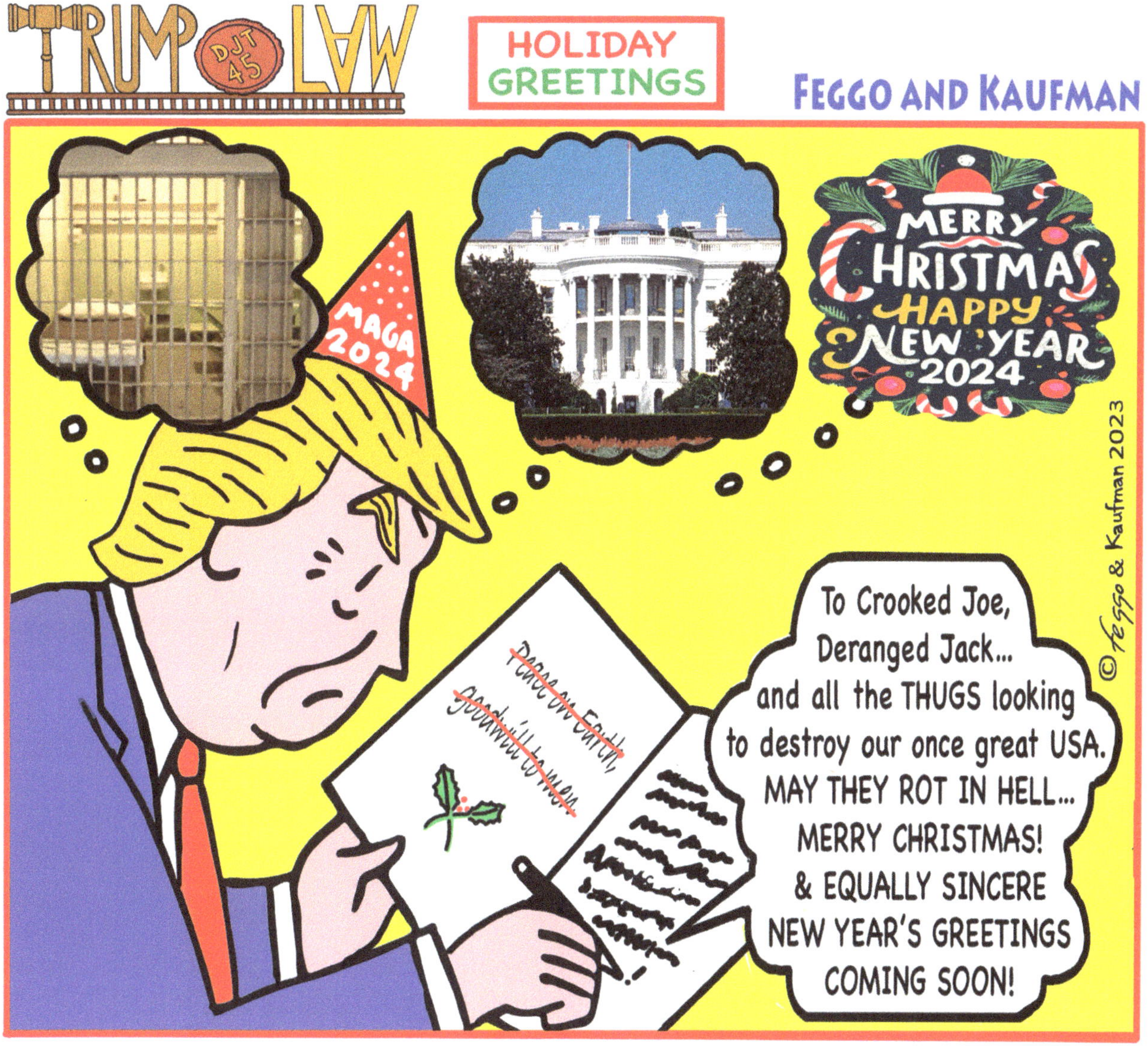

HOLIDAY
GREETINGS

MAGA 2024
MERRY CHRISTMAS HAPPY NEW YEAR 2024
© Feggo & Kaufman 2023
Peace on Earth, goodwill to men
To Crooked Joe, Deranged Jack...
and all the THUGS looking
to destroy our once great USA.
MAY THEY ROT IN HELL...
MERRY CHRISTMAS!
& EQUALLY SINCERE
NEW YEAR'S GREETINGS
COMING SOON!

Here we find Donald Trump in a jolly mood. It seems he's looking on the bright side and celebrating his historic accomplishments! He's setting presidential records for pending criminal cases and for pending civil cases! But it wouldn't be Donald Trump if he had not also built himself a safety net. Here, actually two safe harbors: first, his claim of total immunity for any act taken while serving as President of the United States; and second, as a further backup, he knows he's already stacked the Supreme Court with Justices likely to be on his side!!

Nonetheless, whether Trump's mood will remain jolly, remains to be seen.


Published on X, @henry_kaufman20 and @DavidCayJ, 1/9/24

TRUMP DJT 45 LAW
IT'S A GREAT DAY!
FEGGO AND KAUFMAN
Today and this week I'm setting records: -Hearings in more criminal cases than Al Capone!
-In more civil cases than traffic court after a holiday weekend!
-AND no chance of any problems because -as President- & innocent or not -I'm completely IMMUNE from the law!
-PLUS I've already STACKED the Supreme Court IN MY FAVOR!
© Feggo & Kaufman 2024

As much as we would like to imagine that Donald Trump's bold reach for total immunity from criminal prosecution is as wide a safety net as possible – and for these purposes assuming the Supreme Court might actually even go that far – this cartoon suggests – based on Trump's known proclivity to bite off much more than he can chew – and more than the American polity is able to swallow – that what Trump is really seeking is total impunity (spelled with a "p" rather than a double "mm") with actually no limits on how far he can go in living out his authoritarian fantasies.

The amazing thing is that it's still a live question just how far he will be allowed to go in that direction. He's already up on a tight rope. Can he completely break away from our Nation's democratic gravity?


Published on X, @henry_kaufman20, 2/7/24

TRUMP LAW
DJT 45
IMMUNITY v. IMPUNITY
FEGGO AND KAUFMAN
immunity: protection or exemption from something, especially an obligation or penalty. "the rebels were given IMMUNITY from prosecution."
im·pu·ni·ty: exemption from punishment or freedom from the injurious consequences of an action. "the IMPUNITY enjoyed by military officers implicated in civilian killings."
THIS THEY GIVE. AND CAN TAKE AWAY.
THIS I TAKE! AND WON'T GIVE UP!
© Feggo & Kaufman 2024

Time does not stop – even in a highly consequential, U.S. Presidential election!

We arrived at Valentine's Day and gave our cartoon calendar a little more pizzazz in recognition of the holiday.

264 days to Election Day!

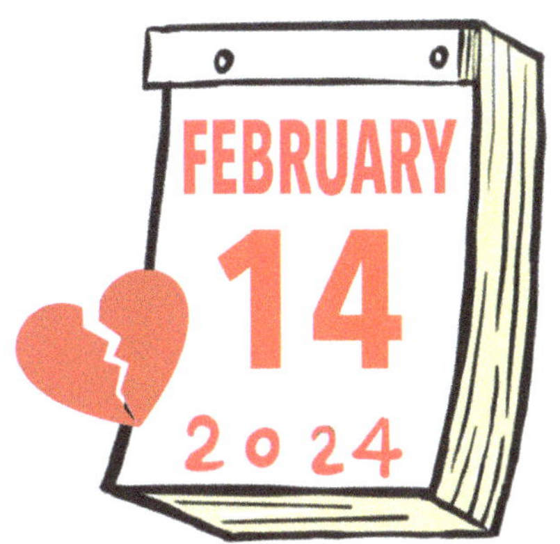

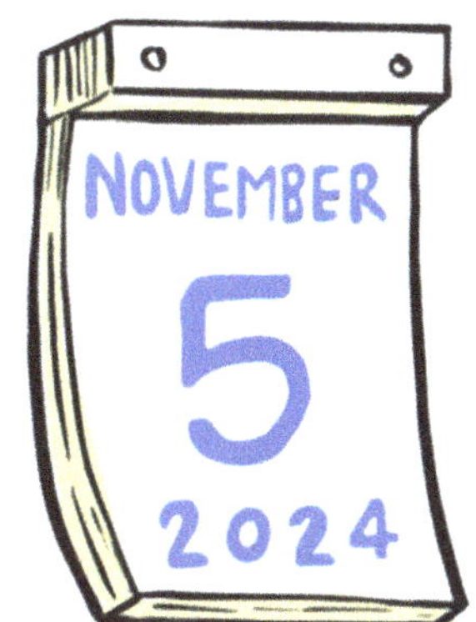

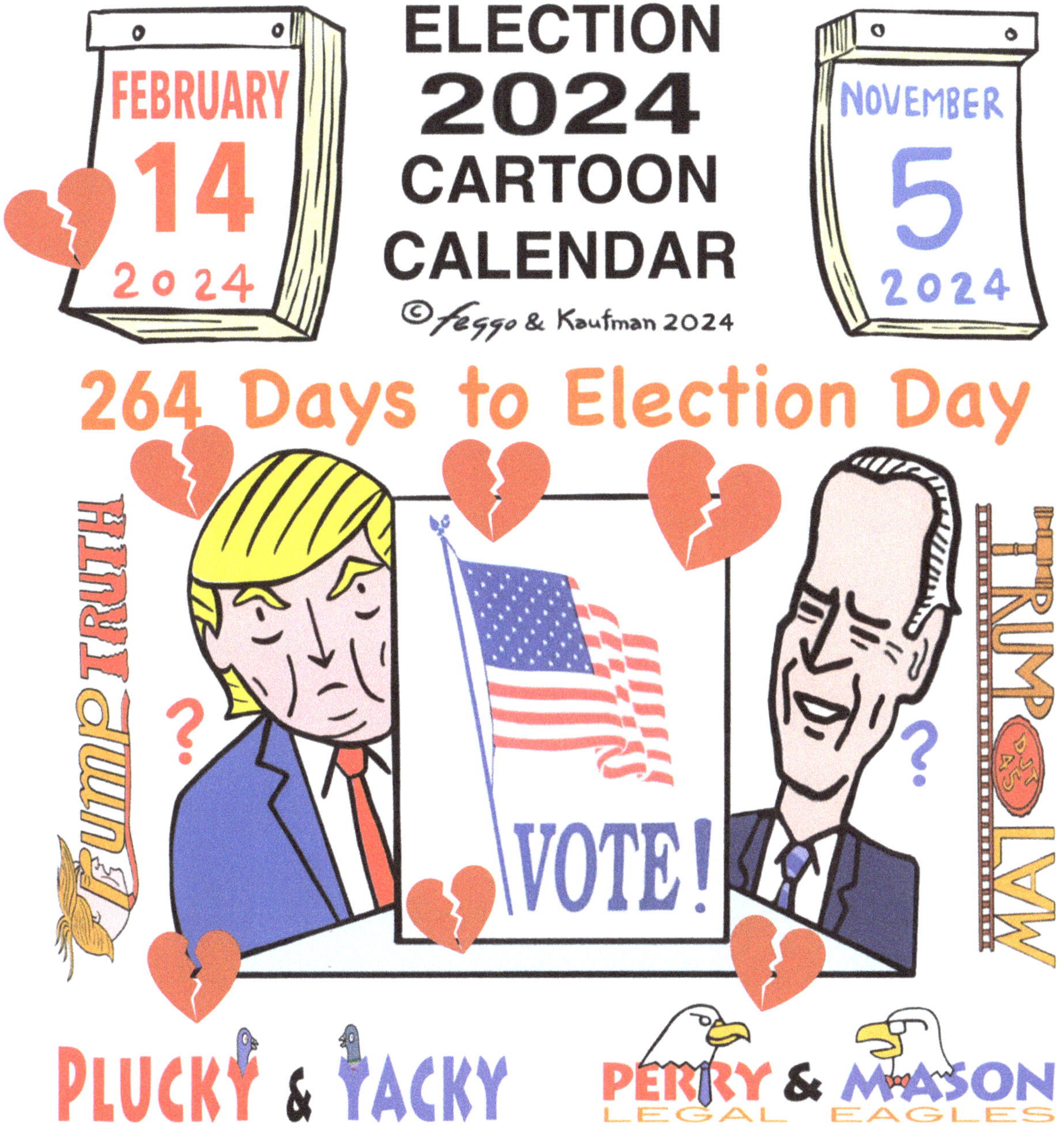
ELECTION
2024
CARTOON
CALENDAR
© Feggo & Kaufman 2024
FEBRUARY
14
2024
NOVEMBER
5
2024
264 Days to Election Day
VOTE!
TRUMP LAW
DJT 45
PLUCKY & YACKY
PERRY & MASON
LEGAL EAGLES

Donald Trump – whether as a young and upcoming landlord at his father Fred's feet, or as a "grown" man confronting what he could consider another readily-resolved business situation – this one simply involving NATO and the fate of the free world! And so, whether it's "business savvy" or "state craft," Donald feels very well equipped to handle it.

See also, "Like Father, Like Son, infra."


Published on X, @henry_kaufman20, 2/15/24 and also on X, @DavidCayJ, 3/21/24.

Also published in *The Nation Online* in its "OppArt" section, 2/26/24.

TRUMP DJT 45 LAW
LIKE FATHER LIKE SON
FEGGO AND KAUFMAN
1970
TRUMP MANAGEMENT
TRUMP VILLAGE
Pay up ya deadbeats!
NATO OTAN
©Feggo & Kaufman 2024
2024

Here, we can evaluate two of Donald Trump's favorite buzzwords ("weaponization" and "election interference") in his crusade to somehow turn in illegal insurrection to his advantage. We've already addressed how it was Trump's "election interference" which came first and what Trump is calling interference is actually the subsequent grinding of the wheels of justice.

As far as "weaponization," from our point of view this is just a dramatic way of explaining how law enforcement will – and it should – move aggressively toward some kind of an appropriate resolution in a case that doubtless stands alone as a one-of-a-kind situation – both from the perspective of law enforcement and from the perspective of civilian participants in the events that day – events which were intended to actually stop the constitutional process of confirming all electoral votes of the states and territories for President of the United States.

Published on X, @henry_kaufman20, 2/18/24

# TRUMP LAW



## FEGGO AND KAUFMAN

In the next spread is the first of six pages of lists of relatively recent cases involving Donald Trump. Many are already aware of Trump's notorious litigiousness, including in his business world over many decades. This is by no means an attempt to create a comprehensive listing of cases which would be in the hundreds if not thousands!

But the following six pages contain just a sampling of some of the cases Trump has been involved in recently. As the reader will see – based simply on the color coding – Donald Trump continues to litigate – win, lose or draw! And so, for a man constantly choosing not only to defend a constant flow of cases against him but also to initiate litigations of all kinds against his political as well as business adversaries, Inc. Trump's claim that he's being persecuted or singled out can be seen as a weak one indeed.

As far as the substantive results of his reason litigations, what follows documents that Trump is by no means always a winner. In fact, he only rarely wins the cases in which he's involved.

NOTE: what follows are six pages of lists of mostly recent cases involving Donald Trump. The majority of those were brought against Mr. Trump. But a substantial number were also initiated by him. Similarly, a majority of the cases listed were lost by Donald Trump. Although he certainly did win some of those cases, with some others still pending. And the pending cases – especially those on page 6, represent mostly the key government cases currently ongoing against Trump, primarily arising out of 2020 election-related types of events, but also some other, post-presidency situations. A handful of the cases have been updated with new developments since being originally posted.

NOTE RE: CODING: For a more detailed explanation of the color coding used in this presentation, see the top of the first page of cases below. Overall, cases coded red have been or are being lost by Donald Trump. Cases coded green have been or are being won by Donald Trump. Cases still in black have not yet been decided.

Pages 1-6 published on X, @henry_kaufman20, 2/23/24

"Weaponization of the Law?" "Election Interference?" or simply
Trumpian "Litigiousness/Lawlessness"? YOU DECIDE!
CODING:
Cases brought by Donald Trump [DJT].
Trump initiated cases won = green / Trump initiated cases lost = red.
Cases brought against Donald Trump [VS].
Cases against Trump lost = red / Cases against Trump won = green.
[UNDECIDED] = no color.
Before 11/8/2016. Selected cases of interest, excluding in particular
litigation involving real estate business deals:

According to a comprehensive Wikipedia entry, from the 1970s until he was elected
President in 2016, Donald Trump and his businesses were involved in something
like 4000 legal cases! Listed here are just a small number of selected litigations pending,
at one stage or another, before Trump was elected President on November 8, 2016.

[VS] In 1973, Trump was sued for violations of the federal Fair Housing
Act in 39 residential buildings in Brooklyn, Queens and Staten Island.
Trump filed a counter-suit which was dismissed as frivolous.
In 1975 the case was settled on undisclosed terms.
In 1978, the Trump Organization was back in court for allegedly
violating the 1975 settlement, which Trump denied.

[VS] In 1985, New York City brought the lawsuit against Trump for
allegedly using improper tactics in order to evict tenants from his
building at 100 Central Park South, which he originally intended to
demolish. After 10 years of litigation a settlement was negotiated
allowing the building to stand in order to be developed as condominiums.

[VS] [DJT] In 1990, in connection with the Trump Taj Mahal casino,
Trump was sued for $2 million for defamation by a business analyst
with whom Trump settled out of court for an undisclosed amount.
Then Trump threatened to sue the analyst's firm which refused to
retract the analyst's published claim that Trump Taj Mahal would fail
before the end of that year, but it did fire the analyst. In fact,
in November 1990, the Trump Taj Mahal declared bankruptcy!
Trump ultimately settled with the analyst on undisclosed terms.

Trump cases won = green / Trump cases lost = red

[DJT] Trump v. O'Brien and Warner Books. (2006) Trump defamation action against author and publisher for allegedly defamatory undervaluation of Trump's net worth. Trial court's grant of summary judgment against Trump affirmed on appeal (2011).

As of Trump's election, 11/8/2016, the following cases were pending – either initiated by or against the incoming President.

[VS] Trump University: Two class actions consolidated with a fraud case against Trump. $25 million settlement paid in November 2016 by Trump toward partial restitution of tuition to thousands of defrauded students.

[VS] Trump Foundation: NYS AG action for improper charitable expenditures,  including contribution to Trump's own 2016 election campaign and for other non-charitable purposes; $2,000,000 penalty imposed on the Foundation; $1.8 million still remaining ordered liquidated. And the Foundation was dissolved.

11/9/16 – 1/20/21: During his presidency, and thereafter, litigation involving Donald Trump continued.

[VS] Inauguration expenditures case: 1/22/20, District of Columbia v. Trump organization and Trump inaugural committee for various overcharges –especially at the Trump Hotel in DC. Case later settled by the defendants for a payment of $750,000 ($400,000 from the Trump organization and the balance of $350,000 from the inaugural committee).

[VS] Three "emoluments clause" cases were pursued against President Trump. Two of the suits (by Maryland and District of Columbia AG's) were dismissed (7/10/19). A third case, pursued by some 200 members of Congress, led by Sen. Richard Blumenthal, proceeded with discovery. However, on 2/7/20, the DC Circuit ruled that the Members of Congress lacked standing. Ultimately, the surviving emoluments clause claims were dismissed as moot by the U.S. Supreme Court (2/22/21) – after Trump was out of office.

**FEGGO & KAUFMAN**

## Trump cases won = green / Trump cases lost = red

[VS] Trump Foundation: NYS AG, 2018. Alleged misuse of charitable funds as illegal contributions to his own 2016 election campaign and for other improper purposes. $2 million dollars in damages imposed on the Foundation. Also, $1.8 million in remaining assets would be donated to proper charities and the Foundation was permanently shut down.

[VS] Federal action in the Southern District of New York, with multiple counts including tax fraud and violation of campaign-finance laws ("hush-money" to "Stormy" Daniels) case ultimately sends Trump personal attorney, Michael Cohen, to jail on a 3-year sentence. Federal indictment in Daniels matter was said to have identified Donald Trump as "unindicted co-conspirator."

#1. (NOTE: Trump was more recently indicted on state charges related to some of the same events. That case is scheduled for trial in March of 2024.(See #5 installment.)

[VS] Early 2019 lawsuit by Michael Cohen vs the Trump Organization for payment of unpaid legal fees. Ultimately, the parties reached an undisclosed financial settlement.

[DJT] December 2021, action by Trump against New York State AG James seeking to enjoin her civil investigation into the Trump Organization's allegedly fraudulent manipulation of property values. James moved to dismiss Trump's suit as an improper attempt to preempt the AG's investigation. In January 2023, Trump withdrew his suit, perhaps out of concern that the assigned Judge Middlebrooks had just fined Trump $1 million for filing a separate frivolous defamation action against Hillary Clinton (See next #4 installment.)

[DJT] Also in relation to AG James's civil fraud investigation, Trump commenced a separate defamation action against a former Trump University student who publicized her negative TU classroom experiences on social media. In April 2015 Trump was ordered to pay the plaintiff and her lawyers just under $800,000 in legal fees and costs.

**FEGGO & KAUFMAN**

Trump cases won = green / Trump cases lost = red

[DJT] Early 2023, Trump sued Cohen for alleged breach of legal trust. In October 2023, Trump dropped the suit ahead of a planned deposition.

[DJT] Trump v. Pulitzer Board. Defamation claim based on the Board's refusal to withdraw the Pulitzer-Prize from winning articles in the New York Times and the Washington Post examining Russian-government interference on Trump's behalf in the 2016 election. Case dismissed as violation of the Publishers' First Amendment rights. Trump had to pay upwards of $400,000 in attorney's fees and interest; payment by Trump may still be pending.

[DJT] Trump v. Hillary Clinton (and FBI officials) for "racketeering." Case ultimately dismissed and $1 million in sanctions assessed against Trump and his attorneys based on "a continuing pattern of misuse of the courts by Mr. Trump..." The judge went on to characterize Donald Trump as "a prolific and sophisticated litigant who is repeatedly using the courts to seek revenge on political adversaries." (S.D. FL, 1/19/23, Middlebrooks, J.)

[DJT] Trump Campaign v. New York Times (and individual reporters), for defamation allegedly caused by an in-depth Times investigative series in 2018 examining Trump's tax returns and related financial matters. One of the Times's key sources was Mary Trump, Donald's niece. She was also named as a co-defendant in the action. The state court judge dismissed the action "as a matter of constitutional law." The judge also ordered Mr. Trump to pay legal expenses and costs incurred by the Times and its reporters. (5/3/23)

[DJT] Trump v. Washington Post (Donald Middlebrooks FL, 3/2020) based on two opinion articles published by the Post in 2019 about the Trump campaign allegedly benefiting from Russian assistance during the 2016 election.

Trump cases won = green / Trump cases lost = red

[VS] State of New York versus Trump Organization. 17 counts of criminal tax fraud related to payment of large "off-the-books perks." Organization found guilty by jury on all counts (12/6/22.) Company CFO, Alan Weisselberg, had pled guilty, turned states evidence and served several months of jail time thereafter.

[VS] E. Jean Carroll v. Trump. A jury in the first trial found that Trump sexually abused and defamed –but did not rape– Carroll. It awarded damages of $5 million. (5/9/23)

[VS] E. Jean Carroll v. Trump. For Trump's additional, post-verdict defamations of Carroll, a second jury –in a case considering damages only– awarded her $83.3 million in compensatory and punitive damages. (1/26/24)

[VS} NYS AG v. Trump: nonjury civil fraud action. $355 million in damages were imposed against Donald Trump by the trial judge, plus interest. In all likelihood –especially given the size of the judgment–this award will be subject to one or more appeals by Trump.(2/16/24)

[VS] In January 2024, a federal judge dismissed a case against Donald Trump and the Trump Organization based on an alleged illegal "multilevel marketing scheme" involving the American Communications Network. The ruling ended the federal case against Trump, although there was some suggestion by the judge that three remaining individual state actions could still be separately pursued against the same defendants, including Trump.

All but one of the following cases remain undecided.

[VS] NYC DA v. Trump: alleged criminal falsification of financial records related to the payment of "hush money" to Stormy Daniels. Jury trial scheduled to begin 3/25/24.

[VS] Georgia v. Trump: state criminal election interference /RICO case against numerous alleged co-conspirators, including Donald Trump.

[VS] U.S. v. Trump (classified documents alleged to have been willfully retained at the former President's club /home); trial currently scheduled for May 20, 2024, although many observers have serious doubts about whether the case will be ready for trial on that date.

[VS] U.S. v. Trump (Jan 6 attempted coup and related, alleged multistate efforts to overturn the result of the 2020 presidential election.) Case to be tried in DC federal court.

[VS] Multi-state attempts to disqualify Trump as a Presidential candidate under the 14th Amendment/Section 3 (persons associated with an "insurrection" or "rebellion"). Colorado's decision in Anderson v. Griswold -disqualifying Trump under 14/3- was argued in the U.S. Supreme Court on 2/8/24. On 3/4/24, the justices unanimously ruled (although in three separate opinions) that the 14th Amendment/Section 3 did not allow the Colorado Supreme Court to bar the former president from the state's primary ballot for President.

[VS] Blassingame and Hemby v. Trump, DC Circuit, 12/1/23: consolidated actions by capitol police and members of Congress seeking compensation from Trump for injuries inflicted during January 6 riot; Trump motion to dismiss based on unrestricted Presidential immunity has been denied and the case remanded for further proceedings.

[DJT] Trump v. Simon & Schuster and Bob Woodward based on an audiobook of interviews with President Trump. Trump claims to be seeking $49 million in damages.

Remember that weekend, toward the end of February earlier this year (2024), when Donald Trump really, really seem to be losing it. Many of his comments were not making sense (even more than usual)! And as he went on and on the word that unavoidably came to mind – and not just ours, many minds – was "rambling." Trump was – really! – A "Ramblin' Wreck."* So this cartoon is what – pretty much inevitably – followed in the hands of our wonderful artist Feggo.

*Not all that many people know that there is actually in existence a "Ramblin' Wreck!" Is from Georgia Tech University!! Lyrics of the fight song ("I'm a Ramblin' Wreck from Georgia Tech"), was said to have first appeared in 1908. But it's actually even older than that! It apparently dates back to a baseball game with Georgia in 1892. The song was even sung on the Ed Sullivan show, in 1953, reaching a television audience of approximately 30 million viewers! Yes, folks, that was what was known as a "national television audience!"

The Ramblin' Wreck is actually a 1930 Model A Ford! It serves as the official mascot of the Georgia Institute of Technology that, evidently, does still run. Ever since September, 1961 the Wreck has led the Georgia Tech team onto the field and it has done so ever since for every home football game!


Published on X, @henry_kaufman20 and also @DavidCayJ, 1/9/24

# TRUMP LAW

Ramblin' Wreck

## FEGGO & KAUFMAN

As someone who frequently follows the United States Supreme Court – closely – I have to confess that, although I have abundant respect for the Court, this cartoon does reflect my genuine view that the Court's scheduling of its hearing in the Jan6 case was a terrible decision given all of the surrounding circumstances and the public's huge and overriding need to know and understand – once and for all – whether Donald Trump did or did not win the 2020 presidential election – and if he did not, whether he knowingly lied about the 2020 election result? In our humble opinion, that is the only way citizens of the United States – on both sides – can go into the polling booth on November 5 and cast an informed ballot as to who should serve as the 47th President of the United States.

The resolution of these issues is of overriding importance to the American people. It simply cannot await some later resolution after the 47th president has been elected. Only Donald Trump in American history has conceived as a possibility that the losing candidate could somehow retain – or achieve – office under such circumstances. And that cannot possibly be any way to run a great Nation!


Published on X, @henry_kaufman20, 3/1/24

TRUMP DJT 45 LAW
JUSTICE DELAYED
FEGGO & KAUFMAN



Why bother to rush?
There will be plenty of time after the 2024 election
to figure out whether Trump believed
the 2020 election was rigged and stolen.
Do the voters really need to know this in advance
of the 2024 election?? Would that
really influence voters one way or another?
© Feggo & Kaufman 2024

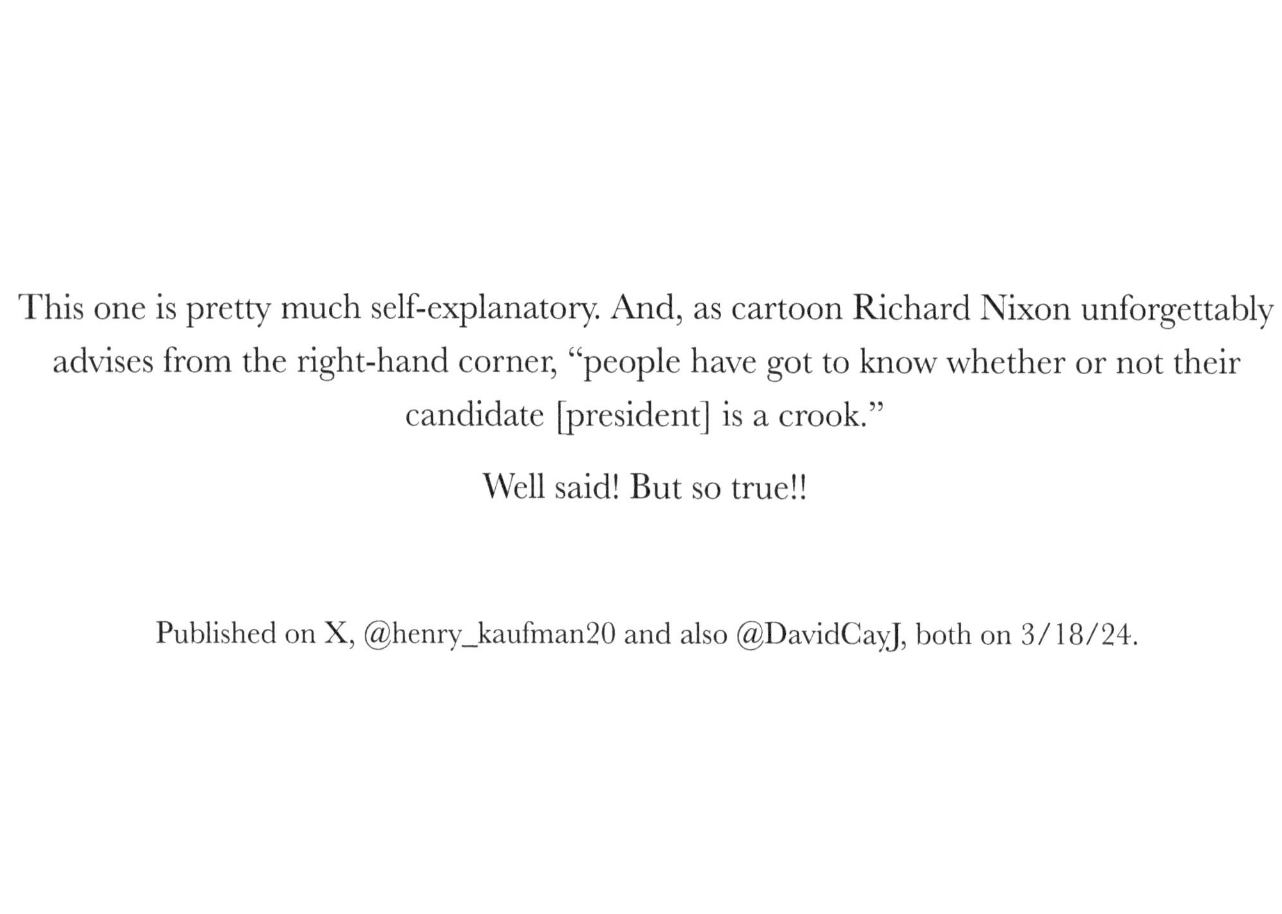

This one is pretty much self-explanatory. And, as cartoon Richard Nixon unforgettably advises from the right-hand corner, "people have got to know whether or not their candidate [president] is a crook."

Well said! But so true!!

Published on X, @henry_kaufman20 and also @DavidCayJ, both on 3/18/24.

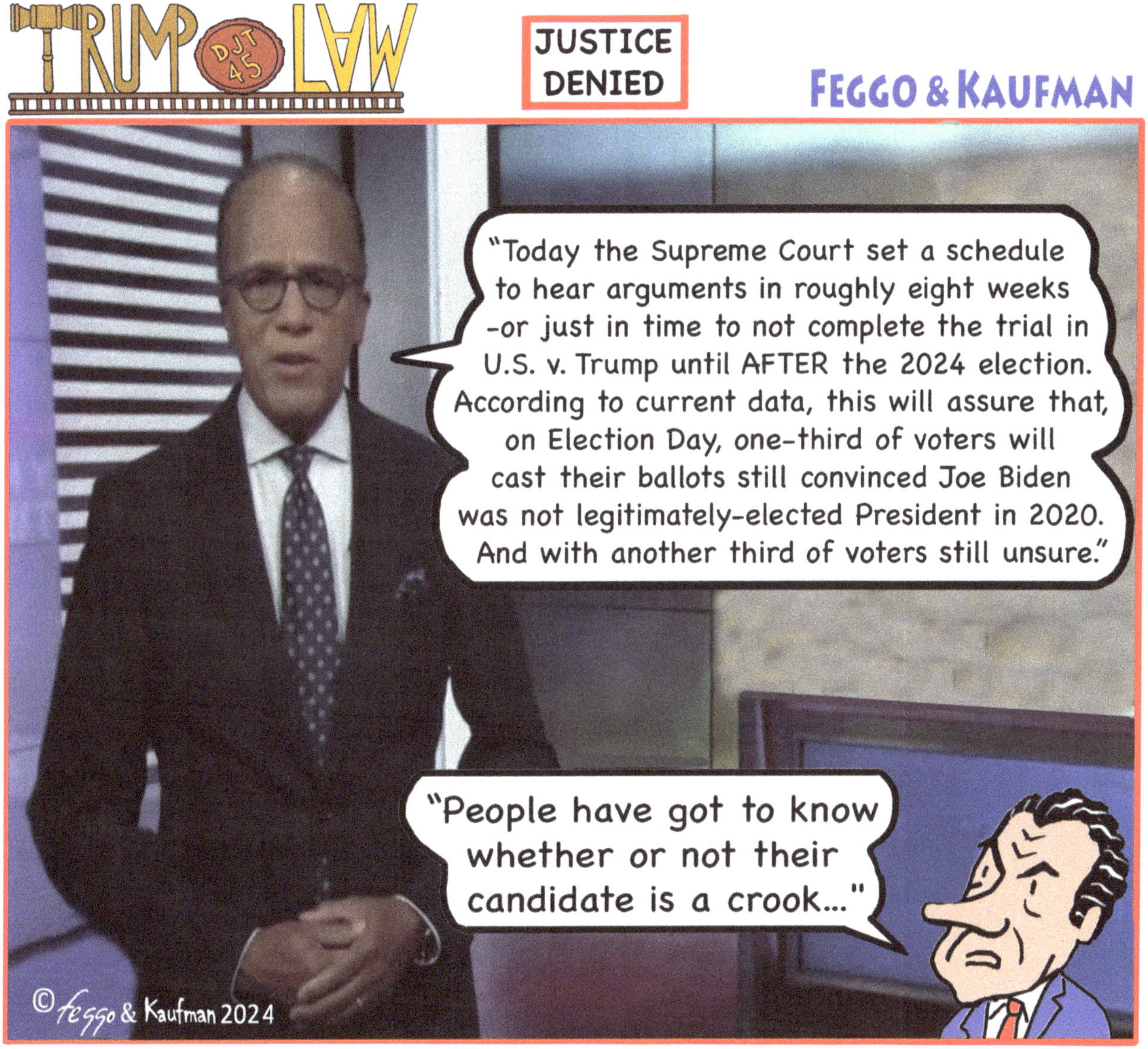

# TRUMP LAW



## FEGGO & KAUFMAN

A WARNING! THIS CARTOON IS HARSH AND UNREPENTANT.<br>
And, it is admittedly an imaginary re-creation of events.

Much ink has already been spilled on the arguably shocking ethical lapses reflected in Justice Clarence Thomas's recent failures to recuse himself in cases involving the Jan6 insurrection at the Capitol. A situation – as most readers probably know – where Justice Thomas's wife, Ginni, was undeniably involved in aspects of that event and its planning! Indeed, she is known to have communicated with the White House, on any number of occasions, about President Trump's efforts to overturn the official results of the 2020 presidential election.

In this cartoon, no prisoners are taken. We savage Justice Thomas as we imagine him accepting his wife Ginni's extreme position when she argues that Donald Trump is a great man who should be reinstalled into office.

Finally, we also imagine Special Counsel, Jack Smith, urging reconsideration because – it is to be hoped – no such situation will arise again in American Presidential politics for another 250 years.

Published on X, @henry_kaufman20, 3/12/24

TRUMP LAW
DJT 45
VINTAGE WINE
FEGGO AND KAUFMAN

I really worry about delaying Trump's Jan6 trial until after Election Day. People need to know the truth.

My Ginnie says: "who are we to rush and judge this extraordinary man? We've seen that only he can make our country great again. The next insurrection can apply the lessons we've learned."

But that could be another 250 years!

My Ginnie says: "practice will make perfect for the next coup, whenever it comes!"

© Feggo & Kaufman 2024

This is another cartoon highly critical of the United States Supreme Court. In which we attempt to explain to the Court – illustrated with picketers and their signs – why and how urgent it is for the voting public to know whether or not the 2020 election was actually "rigged and stolen" – and, if so, by whom and for whom?

Our final cartoon in this book will present a detailed calculation of exactly how much delay can be laid at the feet of the Supreme Court in relation to whether or not the case of United States v. Donald Trump can be tried to verdict BEFORE the 2024 election.


Published on X, @henry_kaufman20 and @DavidCayJ, 3/18/24

TRUMP LAW
DJT 45
VOTERS NEED TO KNOW
FEGGO & KAUFMAN
Voters need to know -BEFORE ELECTION DAY!- Is this true or false?
With no trial, Trump's lies will keep damaging U.S. elections!
U.S. says Trump "KNOWINGLY LIED" that 2020 Election was "stolen."
With no trial, millions will still believe 2020 Election was stolen!
With no trial, Biden's 'legitimacy' will still be questioned!
Court is slowing trial by months! WHY?
WHAT ARE YOU NINE WAITING FOR????
© Feggo & Kaufman 2024

Thoughtful American citizens must acknowledge that defeated former 45th President, Donald Trump, could be playing the biggest April fools* trick in our Nation's history. Harsh? Not necessarily!

The more difficult question is whether the (potentially) great citizens of this Nation will wake up to the danger at hand, on or before Election Day, November 5, 2024.

SO LET US PRAY!

*If the reader looks closely, she will detect a small but amusing detail added to President Trump on this page of the Election Cartoon Calendar for April 1, 2024.

Published on X, @henry_kaufman20, 4/1/24

# ELECTION 2023-2024 CARTOON CALENDAR

©feggo & Kaufman 2024

## 218 Days to Election Day

April fool.

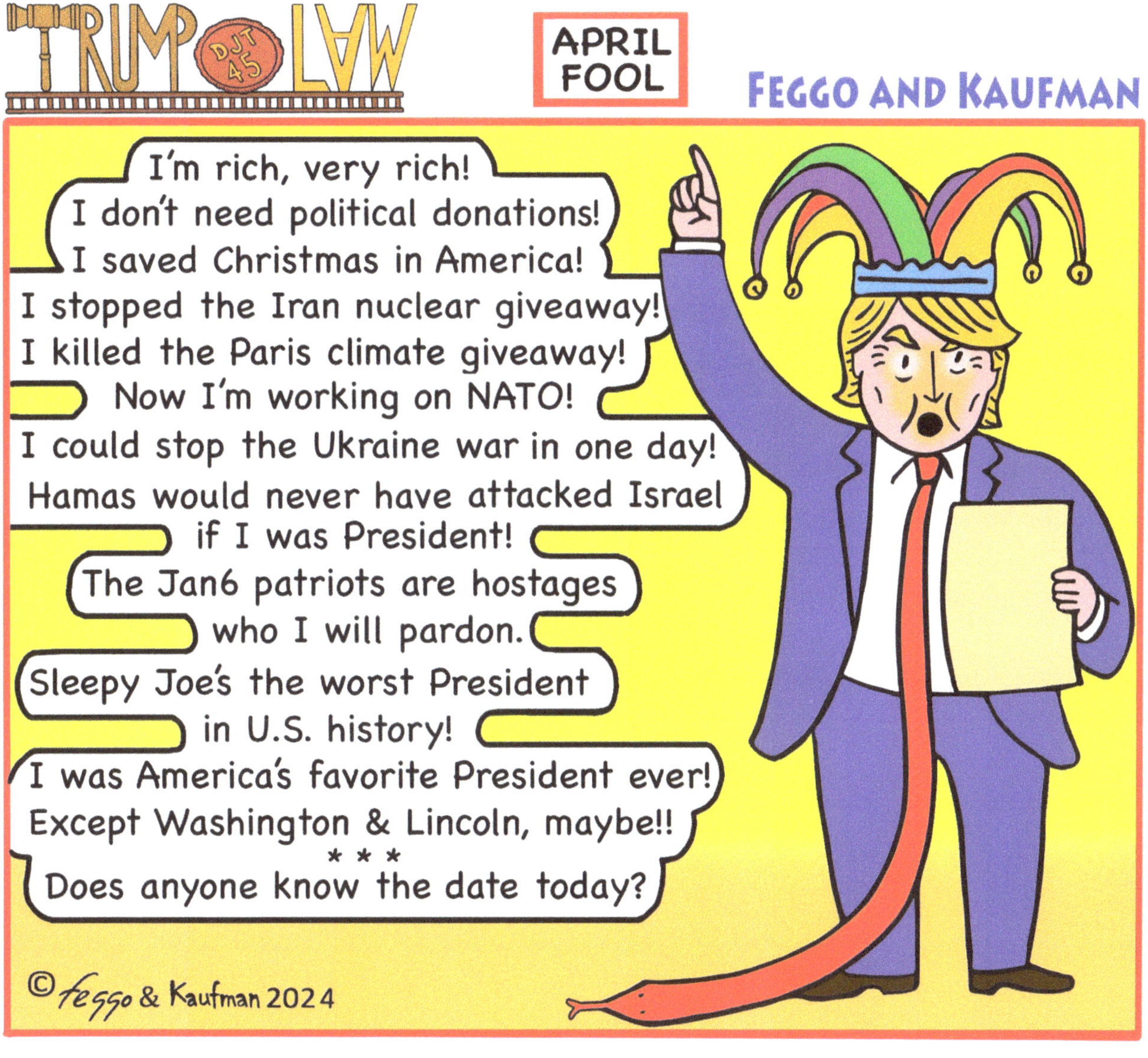

TRUMP LAW
DJT 45

APRIL
FOOL





I'm rich, very rich!
I don't need political donations!
I saved Christmas in America!
I stopped the Iran nuclear giveaway!
I killed the Paris climate giveaway!
Now I'm working on NATO!
I could stop the Ukraine war in one day!
Hamas would never have attacked Israel
if I was President!
The Jan6 patriots are hostages
who I will pardon.
Sleepy Joe's the worst President
in U.S. history!
I was America's favorite President ever!
Except Washington & Lincoln, maybe!!
* * *
Does anyone know the date today?
© feggo & Kaufman 2024

When you think very clearly about what the US Supreme Court has – thus far – done with Trump's big reach for "total immunity," in the case of United States v. Donald Trump, it's very hard to understand why the Court has already delayed consideration of U.S. v. Trump for more than four months. Do they not at least understand that the case MUST be tried to a verdict before Election Day! This is for the obvious reason that the many millions of remaining election doubters or deniers, will finally be exposed to the real evidence that the 2020 election was neither rigged nor stolen!


Published on X, @henry_kaufman20, 4/20/24

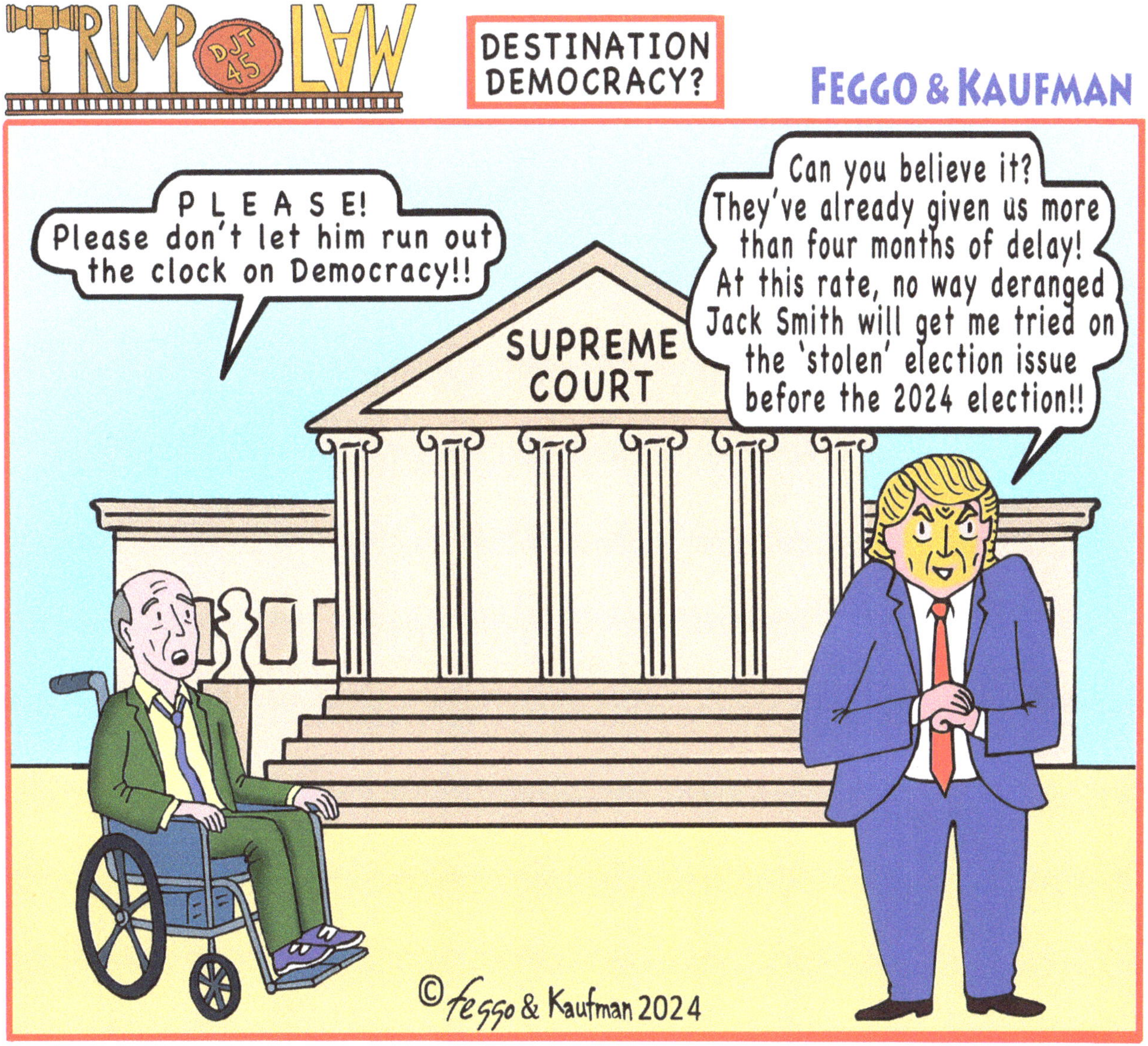

TRUMP LAW
DJT 45
DESTINATION DEMOCRACY?
FEGGO & KAUFMAN
PLEASE!
Please don't let him run out the clock on Democracy!!
SUPREME COURT
Can you believe it? They've already given us more than four months of delay! At this rate, no way deranged Jack Smith will get me tried on the 'stolen' election issue before the 2024 election!!
© feggo & Kaufman 2024

In the Introduction we reflected on how long we've been at work on our Trump cartoons – Book #1 (TrumpTruth) and now this Book #2 (TrumpLaw). During that second period, almost all of our cartoons were conceived and drawn in the context of Trump's extraordinarily early 2024 presidential announcement and campaign. And of course that is not to mention all of the various criminal and civil cases against Trump, announced during that period. We had to recognize that Trump refers to these legal cases as "election interference." And as we've explained – we consider the post hoc legal cases as having actually been started by Trump's election interference, and not the other way around. To be clear, and to avoid sugarcoating, we respectfully submit that all but the brain-dead – or those simply unwilling to think – can understand that Trump's highly-questionable activities came first! And they came before standard legal remedies and procedures were fully considered and applied. And if these formal legal safeguards represented "Election Interference," then what?

So here – finally – we arrive at the one event portrayed in this book that has not yet occurred, but that presumably will happen – just as the moon rises and the sun sets (with or without the hindrance of any total eclipse).

As we think ahead to November 4 – depicted on the following page and denoting a single day before the 2024 presidential election (early and mail-in voting not included) – we can and should ask ourselves whether we will have done all that we could to make voters' stark choices clear. Does a majority of this great nation really want to embark on Donald Trump's promise of a dark and overwhelmingly negative agenda of divisiveness, retribution and a dismantling of our heretofore honored and honorable American democratic experiment?

Or, we can try to imagine what it will feel like on Election Day 2024. Obviously we cannot know for sure. But there is one thing we can know. And that is how hugely important it will be to at least be able to say to ourselves, and those of like mind, that we did everything we possibly could to make our voices – and our votes – heard and counted on this tumultuous occasion.


Henry Kaufman
Felipe Galindo Feggo

# ELECTION 2023-2024 CARTOON CALENDAR

©feggo & Kaufman 2024

# 1 Day to Election Day

# Also Available Online!

A very funny collection of political cartoons created to focus a spotlight on political developments in the late 2020 Presidential campaign.

"A trenchant and artful presentation in a medium that is perfect for getting to the core of who Donald really is."
— *Dr. Mary L. Trump*

www.ingramcontent.com/pod-product-compliance
Lightning Source LLC
Chambersburg PA
CBHW040141110726
48005CB00018B/2606